1 + 1 = 100

Achieving Breakthrough Results Through Partnerships

Rick Pay

BEP BUSINESS EXPERT PRESS

1 + 1 = 100: Achieving Breakthrough Results Through Partnerships

First published in 2017 by
Business Expert Press, LLC
222 East 46th Street, New York, NY 10017
www.businessexpertpress.com

ISBN-13: 978-1-63157-499-3 (paperback)
ISBN-13: 978-1-63157-500-6 (e-book)

Business Expert Press Supply and Operations Management Collection

Collection ISSN: 2156-8189 (print)
Collection ISSN: 2156-8200 (electronic)

Cover and interior design by Exeter Premedia Services Private Ltd., Chennai, India

First edition: 2017

10 9 8 7 6 5 4 3 2 1

Printed in the United States of America.

$$1 + 1 = 100$$

This book is dedicated to my wife, who encouraged me to write it and gently pushed me to complete it. It is also dedicated to Paige McKinney, who helped improve my thinking on the subject, patiently edited the work, and made it a much better book.

Abstract

1 + 1 = 100 guides readers through developing, implementing, and maintaining close relationships within their own company (with employees, design engineering, product development, sales and marketing, operations, and supply chain) as well as outside (with suppliers, customers, and the community). By avoiding overreliance on cost reduction measures and instead developing partnerships, the company and its partners can achieve world-class profitability and cash flow.

For more than 30 years, the focus in industry has been to improve productivity and cut costs using approaches like Lean Thinking, World Class Manufacturing, Reengineering, Strategic Supply Chain strategies, and offshoring. Unlike the techniques that these process improvement methods espouse, partnerships go beyond correcting mistakes or solving problems; they entail looking at the big picture and building on each partner's strengths, making breakthrough results possible for all stakeholders in the relationship.

1 + 1 = 100 speaks directly to operations and supply chain executives in manufacturing and distribution environments, but the concepts are essential for all members of the executive team in any industry that has an operations component and suppliers.

Keywords

accountability, agility, business value, capabilities, collaboration, commitment, competitive advantage, continuous improvement, cost reduction, culture, distribution, implementation, innovation, JIT, key performance measures, manufacturing, memo of understanding, metrics, operations, operations discipline, partnership, problem solving, process improvement, productivity, quality, reshoring, results, strategy, supplier, supplier partner program, supplier score cards, supply chain, sustainability, teams, teamwork, total cost of ownership, trust, vendor managed inventory, vision

Contents

Foreword
by Alan Weiss

My first view of a "partner" was watching an old black-and-white television and the great western shows of the age. The Lone Ranger had Tonto. Roy Rogers and Dale Evans were partners. Gabby Hayes seemed like a perpetual candidate for whoever needed a partner at the moment. They pronounced it "pardna."

There were nonhuman partners. Rusty and Rin Tin Tin. Lassie and Timmie. Asta was the buddy of Nick Charles (*The Thin Man*). Pad Brady appeared in Roy Rogers's movies with his partner—a jeep called "Nellybelle." More recently, *Star Wars* has provided C-3PO and R2-D2 from the outset.

We hear of "partners in crime" both in fact and colloquially. "Life partner" has entered the lexicon to indicate two people living as a committed couple. We hear of "limited partners," "full partners," and "minority partners." A consulting or law firm can have scores of partners, but the key is to be a "named partner," with your name on the door and letterhead. These can be ephemeral. Merrill Lynch Pierce Fenner and Smith eroded to Merrill Lynch, and today they have been subsumed by the Bank of America.

Traditionally, we've viewed "partners" as people involved in business operations on large or small scales who share investment, risk, and profit. We partnered as kids running the never-successful lemonade stands. We've partnered as adults, many of us, in business and investments.

Most recently, partnering has become a strategy with suppliers and customers for successful business. This may include supply chain, sales, finance, R&D, manufacturing, and almost any other aspect of the operations. This can be brilliant (doctors and pharma collaborating on the most efficacious treatments) or calamity (Mercedes "merging" with Chrysler and almost destroying it in the process).

Rick Pay has seen this process in all its dimensions from both sides of the desk. He shows the distinctions between a Wal-Mart putting pressure on suppliers to reduce costs for the sake of its own profit and Supra taking great strides to make itself and its partners mutually successful.

What's happening in your business, whether it's closely held, a division of Fortune 500, a nonprofit, a government agency, or an educational institution? Are you partnering or are you in a zero-sum game where someone has to lose in order for you to win? Rick shows you in the pages that follow how to create a whole that is exponentially greater than the sum of the parts.

So, read on to determine how to leverage your business. Learn how to create alliances and not barriers. I think Rick's approaches are essential to your success. And it probably also wouldn't hurt to get a dog.

Alan Weiss, PhD

Author, *Million Dollar Consulting: The Professional's Guide to Growing A Practice, Million Dollar Maverick: Forge Your Own Path to Think Differently, Act Decisively, and Succeed Quickly*, and over 60 other books

Introduction

I believe strongly in partnerships and their ability to provide everyone with meaning and success in their lives. I believe that partnerships make better products, better relationships, and better results for customers, suppliers, companies, and all their stakeholders. I haven't always felt this way. It wasn't that I didn't believe in partnerships but that I simply never thought about them. Then I took an executive position in a middle-market company and everything changed.

Before I held that position, I was a consultant in a Big 8 (at the time) consulting firm and, later, a partner at a local firm. We specialized in IT system selection, World Class Manufacturing, business process improvement, and productivity improvement. I never thought much about the human aspects of what I did; my job was to improve the business and deliver excellent methodology.

When I started working as VP, Operations, for the first time I really focused on people. I had never directed employees, and suddenly I was in charge of over 70 of them: people with families and aspirations who wanted to do a good job and make a living. I was also in charge of our relationships with our suppliers. They too had aspirations and families to support and wanted their businesses to be successful. In many cases, they were used to being beat up by their customers and developed a typical "us versus them" attitude. As a member of the executive team that led the entire organization, I saw that working together to improve our business was more effective and more fun than the constant turf battles that were common in the companies that I used to consult with.

Partnerships seemed like an obvious way for everyone to achieve new levels of performance. In a partnership, the whole is greater than its parts; 1 + 1 is much more than 2. If partnerships are developed and strongly supported, 1 + 1 can be 100 or more. Now I use the concepts of partnerships in all of my consulting work because it provides my clients with breakthrough results. Partnerships are much more than collaboration. This book provides many examples of partnerships that achieved extraordinary results with customers, suppliers, internal organizations, and the community.

CHAPTER 1

It's Not What You Think

What It Means to Be a Partner

Partnerships benefit both parties, creating a win/win relationship that gives both parties the opportunity to achieve success beyond what they could do alone. Partnerships are founded on an abundance mentality in which the partners help each other improve because one side's success benefits everyone involved. True partnerships offer many advantages:

- World-class pricing and competitiveness
- Greater profitability for both parties
- More flexibility and agility
- Enhanced quality
- Increased return on assets
- A feeling of teamwork and success
- Pride in results

Collaboration is a popular trend, but collaboration stops short of a true partnership. The technical definition of collaboration is "the act of working with someone to produce or create something," in other words, working together toward a joint outcome, but working together may not provide a well-balanced outcome resulting in a win for both sides. Collaboration is certainly a worthy thing, but partnerships provide world-class success for the long term.

Marriage Versus Playing the Field

The best partnerships involve a small number of very close relationships. For instance, many companies have several suppliers for a given material category in an attempt to reduce costs through competition or to reduce risk through redundancy. Unfortunately, this introduces variation, which often cancels out the benefits of cost reduction and risk mitigation. The key in any kind of partnership is to understand that the other party is human and has human desires for success, family, peace, and opportunity. Treating them as partners rather than as opponents yields long-term relationships and spectacular results.

The foundation for partnerships is trust, relationship, and commitment. As Alan Weiss says in his book *Million Dollar Consulting: The Professional's Guide to Growing A Practice*, trust is the firm belief in someone's reliability, truth, credibility, and conviction.[1] Trust comes from

- Knowing that the other party has your best interest in mind as well as their own
- Understanding that the other party has the technical capability to do what the partnership needs done
- Knowing that when the going gets tough, both partners will work together to overcome the difficulty
- Believing that the partner is committed
- Knowing your partner will treat confidential information appropriately

Trust is gained by spending the time with your partners to get to know them and understand their background, experience, capability, and past performance. As in any marriage, if trust is lost, it is very difficult to get back. I visited supplier partners frequently, had lunch with other inside company executives, occasionally played golf with them, and went to their location to get a feel of how they perform.

It is important to take the time to set the foundation for the relationship by reaching conceptual agreement on mutual objectives and by setting measures so that both sides know how they are doing. Conceptual agreement is more than just agreeing on a few points; it is a mutual understanding of objectives and measures.

Supra Products was a small company that made lockboxes used by real estate agents, homeowners, car dealers, and for industrial applications.

---

[1] Weiss (2016).

The company had been in business for many years and grew nicely during that period, but margins were small and competition was tough. The company then decided to pursue a world-class manufacturing philosophy including partnerships with suppliers, customers, and employees. There was a significant change in culture as the company sought out win/win opportunities for all of the stakeholders. The results were nothing short of spectacular:

- Growth of over 400 percent in five years
- Profit before tax growing from 0 percent to over 20 percent
- Inventory turns over 15
- Employee productivity improvement of 77 percent
- Eventual sale of the company for five times its starting value

One of my better clients, Alaska Communications, implemented a supplier partner program over a two-year period. They recently announced a 12 percent stock price increase they attribute partly to their partnerships. My client increased margins, improved service levels, and significantly improved their cash flow. At the same time, their supplier grew their business significantly and increased their own margins. Both companies' performances rose to world-class levels and the value of their businesses rose. The return on investment (ROI) on the partnerships was huge.

Reaching Out and Reaching In

It's time to expand our notion of partnerships to include relationships with suppliers, customers, and the community, as well as relationships within the company.

For an example of an external relationship that is clearly *not* a partnership, let's look at Wal-Mart. As part of its campaign to be more competitive in the marketplace, Wal-Mart puts pressure on its suppliers to cut costs.[2] While increased sales at Wal-Mart could benefit the supplier, for the supplier, the lower prices mean lower profitability. Additionally, the

---

[2] Serena and Ziobro (2015).

change in how the supplier presents its brand to the marketplace could damage its own marketing efforts.

Internal partnerships can bridge the gap between departments. In many companies, functional silos separate departments such as operations and sales, operations and engineering, and operations and accounting. Departmental goals may conflict with the partnerships each department is trying to form, especially with outside interests.

For instance, at Alaska Communications, the purchasing department was trying to improve supplier relationships by paying bills on time, while the accounting department had a conflicting goal of improving cash flow by stretching out the bill pay process. Failure to meet supplier commitments has a tremendous impact on a company's ability to develop external partnerships that reduce costs and improve service. Breaching those walls by transitioning from a collaboration model to true partnerships between departments allows companies to achieve levels of performance beyond anything they've previously accomplished.

Internal partnerships also involve the company and its employees. Open-book management and empowered teams are two methods that have helped many companies build strong partnerships with their employees, which can drive amazing performance.

What Does a Partnership Look Like?

Partnerships can have a dramatically positive impact on business value. Partnerships can in fact earn billions of dollars. A survey of 435 top automotive suppliers found that the Big Three (Ford, General Motors [GM], Ford Chrysler Automobiles [FCA]) had weak supplier relations, costing them over $2 billion in sales in 2014.[3] Those relationships were based on pressure to cut costs using adversarial approaches. Suppliers feared retaliation if they did not comply.

Management wanted to improve relationships and build partnerships, but the internal buyers were trained to negotiate tough deals and cut costs

---

[3] Putre (2015).

wherever possible. Short-term results, key metrics, and quarterly reporting drove the buyer behaviors.

Toyota and Honda, on the other hand, had good supplier relationships and strong partnerships and thus achieved many of their cost targets through "respect for the individual," a basic tenet of the Toyota Production System. Their supplier partnerships were based on trust and respect and focused on total cost of ownership that went far beyond part price.

Since then, Ford has changed their strategy in purchasing to more of a collaborative working relationship, although still short of a partnership, with their suppliers. Savings is not wrung out of the profit margins of the suppliers, and relationships are much more long term. Procurement is partnering internally with design, marketing, sales, and product development to communicate with supplier partners to help them allocate resources to the benefit of both parties.

Culture that supports partnerships starts at the top, with a focus on revenue and customer satisfaction over cost reduction. Often, the cost reduction will come as a result of the partnerships in ways you never expected and that far outweigh the results of normal cost-reduction activity.

In this book, we explore how to develop and maintain partnerships with suppliers, customers, internal departments, employees, and communities. Partnerships are the foundation for world-class performance and provide working relationships that are long term, highly beneficial, and attractive to employees, investors, and other stakeholders. Partnerships feel good, like being on a team of all stars whose performance is beyond belief.

References

Putre, L. 2015. "Weak Supplier Relations Costing Big 3 Automakers, Nissan Billions: Survey." *Industry Week*, May 17 (accessed July 13, 2016).

Serena, N., and P. Ziobro. 2015. "Wal-Mart Ratchets Up Price Pressure on Suppliers." *Wall Street Journal*, 1 April. A1. Print.

Weiss, A. 2016. *Million Dollar Consulting*, 41–45. New York: McGraw Hill Education.

CHAPTER 2

Supplier Partnerships Lead the Way

A few years ago, I asked a buyer from a large high-tech company, "Do you use supplier partnerships as part of your purchasing approach?" She responded, "Of course," as if partnerships were an obvious aspect of purchasing. When I asked, "What do those partnerships look like?" she replied, "If the supplier provides the price, quality and lead time we want, they can be our partner." I asked how their suppliers feel about that, and she answered, "It doesn't matter. There are plenty out there that want to do business with us."

A recent example of this type of vendor relationship is Amazon.com, which accounts for 65 percent of e-book sales in the United States,[1] and its demands that publisher Hachette reduce its e-book prices. This dispute played out in the media throughout 2014, damaging both companies' reputations and making a dent in sales.[2] While the two companies eventually reached an accord, it seems to be an uneasy one.

The Real Definition of a Supplier Partnership

When companies focus on developing partnerships with suppliers, the results in terms of cost, quality, lead time reduction, and overall competitiveness can be astounding. Real supplier partnerships create win/win outcomes that neither party would be able to achieve on their own. Partnerships are based on trust, communication, and both participants' dedication to success.

---

[1] Bercovici (2014).
[2] Streitfeld (2014).

A rapidly growing middle market manufacturing company, Supra Products, had an unexpected opportunity to take significant market share away from its main competitor. The competitor had a major quality problem with their product that rendered them unable to ship for three months. For this product, the initial sale was a system sale with a large installation followed by ongoing replenishment as units wore out. If Supra could ramp up to two or more times their normal output, they could capture a number of the competitor's system sales and decimate their position in the market place.

The catch was that to pull it off, Supra would have to increase their output beyond their known capacity, and (as if that wasn't challenging enough) then ramp back down to normal production levels. This burst mode of production seemed impossible.

In September 1996, Supra explained the opportunity to their employees in production and supply chain. Knowing that the effort would require extraordinary performance from the employees, management created a bonus program to share the increased profit the opportunity would create.

Supra then explained the profit opportunity to its key suppliers. The campaign would stress the suppliers' ability to obtain parts, meet production goals, and still produce high-quality products for rapid customer shipment, but partnerships with key suppliers had been well developed. Conversations occurred not only at the procurement level at Supra and its suppliers, but also at the executive level. It appeared to be a win for everyone if they could pull it off.

The ramp-up started in early October, and demand for the products exceeded the most optimistic forecasts. One supplier was even willing to work on Thanksgiving to help get the product out to meet the demand. Employees at all of the companies came together to meet their goals, with progress displayed at each plant using a United Way thermometer-type graphic. At the peak of the campaign, the partners were producing at three times the normal levels, far beyond their known capacity.

All of the partners supplied an extraordinarily high volume of parts just in time, and in the end, Supra was successful in taking so much market share away from their competitor that the competitor eventually dropped out of the market. By mid-December, production was back to levels slightly higher than normal and employees received big bonus checks just in time for the holidays.

Several things made this success story possible:

- A few key suppliers produced the majority of the parts needed because the company had worked hard to rationalize its supplier base, focusing on a few key partners.
- The lines of communication were open across multiple levels of the organizations.
- Everyone wanted success and profitability for all participants and was willing to work hard for it.
- All parties realized that taking significant business from the competitor would benefit them all, now and into the future.

Supplier partnerships go well beyond basic collaboration, which is defined as "the action of working with someone to produce or create something." Collaboration is simply working with another company toward a joint outcome, often without regard for the deeper impact on people, processes, and profits.

A recent example of what a supplier relationship *shouldn't* look like is Apple and one of their suppliers, as told in a series of articles in *The Wall Street Journal*.[3] Apple selected a supplier, GT Advanced Technologies, to create a screen for their new phones made out of artificial sapphire, a material that was supposed to be harder than glass and less susceptible to scratching and breakage.

Apple agreed to invest in a plant that GT planned to build in Texas to the tune of over $700 million, but to GT's apparent surprise, withheld their final payment of $139 million. GT share prices plummeted and the company eventually filed for bankruptcy. What happened to this collaboration?

There were several indications that this was *not* a true partnership. GT said it could produce a product that would solve the problem of scratched and broken smart phone screens, but, apparently, GT wasn't able to produce the artificial sapphire screens and Apple engineers decided not to use

---

[3] Wakabayashi (2014).

them in their phones. GT struggled with low manufacturing efficiency, and some processes didn't work at all. GT had never produced sapphire screens before, only the furnaces that made the material.

How could Apple not know this? Why didn't Apple engineers and GT engineers work hand in hand toward their shared objective?

Apple withheld payments on the plant due to GT's poor performance. When GT declared bankruptcy, it "surprised" Apple. Apple had been working with GT to keep it solvent, so how could the bankruptcy be a surprise? In the end, GT said that its agreements with Apple were "oppressive and burdensome."

Partnerships are built on a foundation of trust and communication. There might have been trust between Apple and GT (or perhaps just wishful thinking), but there certainly wasn't good communication. Collaboration is a worthy thing, but world-class success requires real partnerships.

Separating the Wheat From the Chaff

The first step in creating supplier partnerships is to rationalize the supplier base. A typical company's supplier base becomes bloated over time and can expand to hundreds or even thousands of suppliers. They use requests for proposals (RFPs) every time they add new products, want to check prices, or order additional parts. Can you imagine the amount of time that goes into preparing, issuing, reviewing, and selecting new suppliers? In addition, any hope for volume discounts and long-term relationships goes up in smoke when companies rely too heavily on RFPs. Many of the best suppliers won't even respond to RFPs, especially if they don't have a previous relationship with the company.

There's a very simple report that can provide a window into the supplier base. It's a list of suppliers in descending order based on either purchase orders (POs) issued year to date or payments made year to date. Most accounting packages include this report in the accounts payable system and it's also typically available as part of the PO tracking system.

What I've found over years of analyzing these reports is that the top five to seven suppliers usually make up about 50 percent of the total spend on materials, with 13 to 20 suppliers usually comprising 80 percent of the total spend, and the rest (often hundreds of suppliers) receive the remaining 20 percent of total materials spending. Keep in mind that the administrative costs (issuing and managing POs, selection, issuing checks, etc.) of working with suppliers in the bottom 20 percent are the same as working with the top suppliers. The broader the supplier base is, the lower the likelihood of volume discounts and the greater the likelihood of quality variation.

The report itself is very simple (see Figure 2.1). The commodity column (second from left) can be particularly revealing, because, typically, there should be only two or three suppliers for a particular commodity, and here lies the opportunity to rationalize the supplier base.

Description	Def. Gen. Prod. Posting Group	2009 Spend	%	
Supplier 1	SEALANTS	$4,449,293.59	37.6	
Supplier 2	SEALANTS	$1,131,805.57	9.6	
Supplier 3	H20 PROOF	$860,510.05	7.3	TOP 3 54%
Supplier 4	COATING	$777,770.77	6.6	
Supplier 5	COATING	$626,684.90	5.3	
Supplier 6	SEALANTS	$524,445.66	4.4	
Supplier 7	H20 PROOF	$337,513.79	2.9	
Supplier 8	SEALANTS	$297,843.40	2.5	
Supplier 9	MISC	$254,993.08	2.2	
Supplier 10	TOOLS	$213,947.78	1.8	TOP 10 80%
Supplier 11	H20 PROOF	$119,318.18	1.7	
Supplier 12	MRO	$182,005.36	1.5	
Supplier 13	SEALANTS	$180,420.36	1.5	
Supplier 14	MRO	$152,167.75	1.3	
Supplier 15	FIRESTOP	$137,602.79	1.2	
Supplier 16	H20 PROOF	$126,592.53	1.1	
Supplier 17	CREP	$121,463.23	1.0	
Supplier 18	MISC	$119,469.52	1.0	TOP 25 $11,249,329.10
Supplier 19	H20 PROOF	$104,529.25	0.9	
Supplier 20	TOOLS	$102,130.40	0.9	
Supplier 21	TAPES	$89,081.25	0.8	
Supplier 22	H20 PROOF	$81,836.68	0.7	
Supplier 23	SEALANTS	$66,539.55	0.6	
Supplier 24	CREP	$59,678.61	0.5	
Supplier 25	MRO	$51,684.78	0.4	

Figure 2.1 Top 25 supplier analysis sample

Channeling the spend from a large number of suppliers into only a few suppliers creates opportunities for volume discounts; many companies save 5 percent to 20 percent by concentrating their business in a few suppliers. Suppliers are often willing to reduce costs based not only on a large order volume for a particular part but also on the total value of the supplier relationship across all of the parts you buy from them.

Occasionally, a particular supplier may provide a totally unique item. In the electronics industry, for example, customers of contract manufacturers often call out specific parts (which come from a specific supplier) that they want on a printed circuit board assembly. There's no alternative and the contract manufacturer must buy that part from that particular supplier even though they make no other purchases from them.

Many companies claim that by having multiple suppliers they're reducing risk by keeping their purchasing options open. A good way to achieve the same result with fewer suppliers is to sole-source parts and dual-source technology. In other words, buy any particular part from just one supplier, thereby consolidating volume and maximizing discounts. Then buy another part—in the same family of parts—from a second supplier. This way, you have relationships set up with two qualified suppliers, so if something happens to Supplier A (or to the supply chain associated with Supplier A, like storms or earthquakes), you can quickly switch to Supplier B.

Supra Products used three aluminum extrusion parts in their product. The company bought all of part 1 from Supplier A and all of parts 2 and 3 from Supplier B. They took advantage of the cost efficiencies of fewer setups and consolidated volume, yet they had relationships with two suppliers so they could quickly switch suppliers if there was an interruption in the supply chain.

Two suppliers are typically sufficient to reduce risk, and three would be the absolute maximum. For example, as you saw in Figure 2.1, the company buys sealants from several vendors. Barring unique items, the company has a big opportunity to consolidate their supplier base, save direct materials costs, and reduce overhead. Because it brings more business to the chosen suppliers, consolidation is a win/win situation.

Selecting Partners for Life

Finding good supplier partners is challenging and it starts with the selection process. A "dating period" is necessary to decide if you want to spend the rest of your life with a supplier partner; getting to know the partner and whether their interests and outlook are similar to yours is vital to a strong and lasting relationship. Supplier partners will help you lower costs, increase quality, and improve service. They'll provide higher operating efficiencies, lower inventory, and shorter cycle times.

The perfect partner communicates effectively and frequently and participates in your design processes to help you make better products that win more customers and profits in the long run. One example of this is Wal-Mart providing detailed sales data to its suppliers to help them create products that will sell in large volume.

In order to satisfy your customers in a competitive and constantly changing market, suppliers must have consistent, high-quality processes and be able to deliver reliably with short lead times. Supplier partners need to be willing to share the risks of the relationship and work closely with you to satisfy your customers. They must be willing to expose their technical capabilities to evaluation and their cost structures to review.

The process starts with your team. Many companies leave supplier selection either to the design engineers or the purchasing group, but there are several players you'll want on your partner selection team:

- Purchasing personnel—contract development, price setting, material flow expectations
- Manufacturing/engineering—review of technical capabilities to be sure that the supplier can maintain the levels of tolerance and quality needed
- Quality—to determine whether the supplier has a system of quality and the ability to meet regulatory requirements
- Finance/accounting—to determine whether the supplier is financially stable and to develop processes for resolving invoice issues and making payments

Together, this team visits the suppliers to make sure they measure up to expectations and to create the foundation for the partnership.

Supplier selection starts with your supply chain designs. Determining where the supplier's materials or services will be used is a key part of the decision-making process. Alaska Communications (ACS) served construction projects all over the state from a warehouse in Anchorage and brought materials up by barge from suppliers in Seattle. When they needed to transfer materials to their satellite warehouse in Juneau (a city that is inaccessible by road), they were shipped from the warehouse in Anchorage—but took a side trip to Seattle first. That's right: Seattle to Anchorage, back to Seattle, then finally to Juneau. Obviously not a very efficient logistics architecture.

With my assistance, ACS worked with their supplier to completely redesign the supply chain. The supplier kitted materials in Seattle and sent them directly to construction projects all over the state, including Juneau. This way, the materials didn't pass through ACS's warehouses, meaning fewer transactions, less time sitting on shelves, and lower handling and logistics costs. In addition, the inventory cycle time was shortened, which helped cut the inventory balance by millions of dollars. Having a supplier partner enabled my client to better serve their construction teams while reducing costs and inventory levels. The supplier got the majority of the construction business in the state. A true win/win relationship.

The Prenuptial Agreement

An attorney once told me that the only reason you need a contract is if you plan to sue someone. While it's important to spell out the expectations, terms, and conditions for a supplier relationship, the resulting contract is often just pages of legalese that no one but your attorney understands. A better way to approach this is to have

1. Standard terms and conditions (T&C)
2. A memorandum of understanding (MOU) between the parties

The T&C was written in the standard language often found on the back of printed POs back in the "old days" when they were multipart forms. The PO can be replaced with a printed or e-mailed document (one page) that refers to standard T&C that you give to the supplier for their files at the beginning of the relationship.

The MOU is something else entirely. It's an agreement between the parties that is normally about four or five pages long. It deals with

- Timing (beginning and ending dates)
- Forecasts and PO process—how POs will be issued, which forecasts the customer will provide, and, most importantly, what the commitment is for blanket POs. It also defines the liability for costs
- Pricing and terms
- Quality expectations
- How nonconforming parts will be managed
- Delivery expectations
- How supplier performance will be measured
- Confidentiality provisions
- Modifications and product changes
- Any special warranties and indemnification

The MOU is straightforward, complete, and partnership oriented. For an example, see Appendix.

Keeping the Relationship Exciting

Many supplier relationships, once launched, drift forward on their own as long as materials show up as ordered and when expected. Over time, the relationship atrophies and begins to decline, just like a marriage that isn't maintained and developed. To stay strong over the long haul, a relationship needs a little dose of excitement. With suppliers, there are three ways to keep things exciting.

First, include suppliers in new product development. Concurrent engineering invites the supplier into the design process early, giving the supplier the chance to suggest materials to increase performance and reduce costs, propose ways to change tolerances to make the product more manufacturable, and help design packaging and other components to improve quality. Concurrent engineering treats suppliers like a valuable resource (which they ought to be), and offers them a peek into your R&D.

Next, get "executive sponsors" involved. Establish relationships between your CEO and CFO and their counterparts at your top 10 suppliers. Involve your head of engineering, your COO or VP, Operations and even your sales and marketing people. In my experience as a VP, Operations, at Supra Products, I'd occasionally ask my CEO to contact the supplier's CEO to work out a difficult issue. They would discuss the issue and its impact on both businesses, and resolution was always quick to follow.

Third, keep multiple communication channels open. For example, hold a supplier day once or twice a year. Bring in all of your top suppliers and inform them what's coming in terms of new products, sales increases, new initiatives that might impact them, and so on. Have your engineering team share new products. Have your VP of Sales present the forecast for the coming year or two. Show the suppliers their future opportunities to increase their business with you and to participate in concurrent engineering processes.

At ACS, during a supplier day event, the suppliers initiated discussions with each other to see how they could work together to better serve their mutual customer. Even though we intentionally put competitors in the room, partnerships began to grow among them. They appreciated the fact that we bought small gifts and lunch for them, with one saying, "No one has ever done that before." The meetings instilled a feeling of camaraderie that yielded benefits like new ideas for material flow, consolidation of parts, and better and cheaper materials.

Supplier partnerships based on a foundation of trust can yield great rewards for both parties. Much more than collaboration, partnerships provide the right products in the right place at the right time at the best possible profit margins. When I was VP of Operations, I used to say that I wanted to be my supplier's most profitable account, while at the same time they provided me with world-class pricing and service: a true partnership.

References

Bercovici, J. 2014. "Amazon Versus Book Publishers, by the Numbers." *Forbes Magazine,* February 10. Web. May 13, 2015.

Streitfeld, D. 2014. "Amazon and Hachette Resolve Dispute." *The New York Times,* November 13. Web. May 13, 2015.

Wakabayashi, D. 2014. "Apple Sapphire Partner GT Advanced Files for Bankruptcy Protection." *The Wall Street Journal,* October 6. Web. May 13, 2015.

CHAPTER 3

Innovative Strategies for Supplier Partnerships

Many companies seek cost reduction from suppliers by simply trying to negotiate better costs, delivery, and terms. Some customers will require a 3 percent to 6 percent cost reduction every year, without having any suggestions as to how that might be accomplished. This chapter explores how to select your supplier of choice for given parts, how to reduce costs by far more than the 3 percent to 6 percent targets set by many companies, how to use innovative approaches to supply chain management that reduce costs exponentially throughout the supply chain, and how to determine when it's wise to take your partnerships global and when to keep them at home.

In my past role as VP, Operations, of a rapidly growing manufacturer, I established a culture of partnership with our suppliers where we expected to be their most profitable account, while they provided us with world-class pricing. How did we do that? By promising that we wouldn't squeeze their profit margins but would instead work *with* them to reduce costs—materials, labor, overhead, quality, freight, and the other costs included in a total cost of ownership (TCO) model.

We began early in the relationship by asking that our supplier partners (usually the top 10 suppliers in total dollar volume—see Chapter 2) give us their complete cost model breakdown so we could see what drove their costs and what we could do to help them reduce *our* costs for materials. My buyers spent time reading *The Wall Street Journal* and other related publications so that they understood the dynamics of costs for the materials they bought. For instance, the buyers who bought printed circuit board assemblies (PCBAs) knew the market benchmarks for profit margin, materials, labor, and so on. We knew at the beginning that the typical industry profit margin was, say, 7 percent, and we started working with that as the minimum for that part. Then, as we worked on cost reduction with the supplier, we would split the savings with them so that each time a reduction was identified, we got half and they got half. It didn't matter who found the savings, it would be split between the parties. Over time, their profits went up and our costs went down.

Whenever we met with the suppliers, which for our top suppliers was usually quarterly, cost reduction was at the top of the agenda. We pored over drawings, looking for opportunities to reduce costs, such as loosening tolerances that were not important to the design performance of the product. We often found that the engineers would call out the same tolerance for most measurements whether it really needed to be that tight or not. Often, some could be loosened, which significantly improved the supplier's ability to build the part for less money. We also considered alternative materials, substitute components, parts they could purchase in greater quantities for all of their customers, and so on. Then, as part of our supplier performance reports, we measured cost reduction and reported it back to the supplier during our reviews.

By working together to become more competitive in the marketplace, the increase in our sales benefited both parties through higher volumes, better margins, improved quality, and reduced scrap. Because we were our supplier's most profitable account, whenever we needed extra support for some reason, like a market opportunity or a design change to help move the technology forward, our suppliers were more than willing to go the extra mile to help us. How did we find suppliers who would do that? We used a technique patterned after the U.S. Air Force Fly-off.

The Air Force Fly-Off

When the U.S. Air Force selects new airframes for fighters, bombers, tankers, and other aircraft, they often use an approach known as the fly-off, in which they provide performance criteria to two selected companies who each build their proposed prototype aircraft; these are then compared through a series of performance tests.

The Air Force actually started this process way back in the 1930s when it was known as the Army Air Corps, for the procurement of post-World War I (WWI) fighters and bombers. There have been more than six generations of fighter aircraft since 1939 when the first jet airplane was developed. There was a period in the 1950s and 1960s when the fly-off fell out of use due to internal disagreements in the Air Force as to the purposes of fighter aircrafts. Should they be bombers, close air support, or interceptors? Then, with the development of the F-15 and, later, the "Lightweight Fighter" (LWF) that became the F-16 and the Navy F-18, the fly-off returned to use.[1]

In materials acquisition, the fly-off model can serve as a way to determine which supplier becomes the primary, or often the sole, source for a given part or assembly. For instance, in the company where I was VP, Operations, two PCBA houses provided parts for us. When a new design was released, we gave it to both suppliers to bid and to provide samples for review. While both met the design requirements, our production personnel noticed basic differences. Often, one supplier's starting costs were very different than the other, or one supplier's quality was different. For instance, we used conformal coat, which encased the PCBA in a plastic coating to allow the product to function outdoors. One supplier spray-coated, while the other dip-coated the conformal coat, which affected how the PCBA was placed into the assembly. Our production personnel noticed the difference as they tried to assemble the product.

Once we chose our primary supplier for a given product, we would buy 60 percent of the product from them and 40 percent from the second supplier. Then, based on quality, delivery, cost reduction, and other subjective factors, we would either flip who the primary supplier was or give the initial supplier more of the volume, until one supplier was the sole source for that particular part. This "fly-off" might take a year. Usually, the second supplier still provided other parts of a similar nature, so we had the risk reduction of dual suppliers with the cost reduction of sole source supply for individual parts.

Our "fly-off" was particularly effective in providing high-quality parts at the lowest possible cost just in time. The supplier gained the benefit of new, high-volume business, while we got world-class pricing with extraordinary performance. It also helped reduce our overhead by reducing the number of purchase orders (POs) and checks issued. The one difference

---

[1] Hallion (1990).

between our "fly-off" and the Air Force Fly-off is that we provided the detailed design to the suppliers so they built technically identical parts, rather than completely different airframes (as in the Air Force) that met a defined need.[2]

Auto Replenishment Systems

Auto replenishment systems go back a long way. Two-bin, *Kanban*, breadman, and other systems have been around since Henry Ford and possibly longer. When Taiichi Ohno created the Toyota Production system, one of the ways he developed level flow was though Kanban. Kanban is a card or signal that indicates when something needs to be done such as a part movement or materials purchase. Vendor-managed inventory (VMI) (also known as supplier-managed inventory) is another widely used technique. It could be argued that material requirements planning (MRP) is also an auto replenishment system, but it's not quite as "automatic" as others.

VMI is just that, a system where the supplier manages your inventory. In more full-featured implementations, the supplier first helps to rationalize the inventory. There's no point setting up a replenishment system for parts that are obsolete or exceptionally slow moving, so the first step is to identify parts with no recent activity and remove them from the process. What's left should be the parts that are used on a more or less regular basis, although high volume isn't required for a successful VMI system.

In VMI, the supplier visits the customer, examines the bins or storage locations to see what's been used, and replenishes the items as needed. It's also known as a breadman system, because in grocery stores, bread is typically resupplied using this process, although I often note that beer is, too, which seems more interesting to me!

VMI is completely different than consigned inventory, although many companies assume that VMI inventory is consigned. Consigned inventory is owned by the supplier until it's actually used, which can cause problems that hurt the partnership. For instance, what happens if the supplier thinks there should be more parts in stock than the customer

---

[2] McChesney (2008).

wants? Perhaps inventory was taken without being transacted, or parts were damaged upon arrival, but there are arguments as to who is responsible. Perhaps a physical inventory reveals discrepancies, but no one knows why. All of these and other issues can cause bad feeling between the parties, which could lead to the demise of the partnership.

Another interesting problem is whose insurance covers the consigned parts in the event of a disaster such as a fire or a flood. They're still owned by the supplier, but they're in your warehouse and under your theoretical control, so whose insurance covers the parts? In my opinion, a well-run VMI system should have such high inventory turns that consignment has little benefit and just isn't worth the potential problems between the parties. When parts arrive in the bins, ownership should transfer or the parts should be expensed.

VMI is most often used for fasteners and packaging, but I've seen very successful systems used for electronics, cable, wood, steel plates, and many other items. The key to a well-run system is to think just in time with high turns. Many companies don't support VMI because they believe the suppliers stuff the bins, leaving them stuck with too much inventory. There's actually a very easy fix to that—make the bins smaller. If VMI is founded on a strong partnership, many of these problems simply won't occur, but like any process, it needs to be managed.

Kanban systems, based on a signal or trigger for replenishment, can be used both internally and externally. In supplier partnerships, they can be used to replenish just in time, yielding very high inventory turns and low levels of stock-outs. When I was VP, Operations, other than VMI parts, we had 100 percent Kanban replenishment with our suppliers. It resulted in turns over 17 with 99 percent demand fulfillment.

Kanban also helped with seasonal parts management issues. For instance, many of our zinc parts were produced almost 1,000 miles away and had to go over a pass in the mountains, which could be closed in the winter due to avalanches. My production managers simply added an extra card to the Kanban mix in November that increased inventory and then removed it in April to bring inventory back to the ideal quantity.

Once again, Kanban must be managed to work effectively. Someone needs to keep an eye on demand to know that the quantities are set correctly, and if anything goes wrong, alarms need to sound immediately.

For instance, Kanban size is calculated based on average usage lead time. If parts are late, a signal needs to go to the buyers to contact the supplier to find out what happened and when the parts will arrive; otherwise, a stock-out could occur.

Alaska Communications (ACS) had a series of retail outlets for the sale and service of cell phones. Customers could go to the retail store to select a phone from the large selection, chose accessories for the phones, and sign up for the service to support the phone. The stores had a hard time keeping many models in stock and managers complained that stock-outs were hurting sales, so operations set up a Kanban system between the central warehouse and the stores that triggered replenishment. An individual visited each store several times a week to deliver products and pick up the Kanban cards that signaled further replenishment when a bin was empty. They set up a simple two-bin Kanban system that was incredibly effective, dramatically reducing inventory while increasing customer service to the highest levels in recent memory.

ACS also used a variation of VMI they called vendor-managed delivery. This worked in two completely different applications, one to refill technician trucks and one to deliver materials to construction locations. They had a fleet of over 120 technician vehicles for business and residential service and installation, which carried a wide selection of parts and wire. Every day, the technicians visited the warehouse parts counter, turned in their list of replenishment parts, and then went to the coffee machine while the parts were pulled. Then they restocked their trucks before leaving to start their service calls. This process often took 45 minutes, and each technician had his or her favorite parts, which caused significant stock-keeping unit (SKU) inflation over time.

Partnering with a supplier who made most of the components, the company developed suitcase-like containers with pigeonholes for the parts (Figure 3.1). The parts were standardized in the containers, which had the added benefit of reducing the number of SKUs in inventory, since each technician had his or her favorite brand of parts and over time, this resulted in significant SKU inflation. By limiting the parts in the box, the number of SKUs were dramatically reduced, which saved both money and floor space. Now the technicians could simply exchange their two cases for freshly stocked ones and return to their trucks. Total time, with

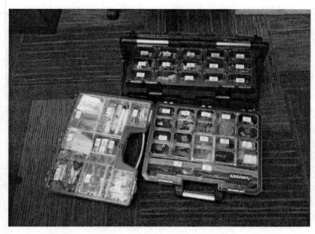

Figure 3.1 ACS parts kit

coffee, was five minutes or less. That time savings across the 120 trucks led to remarkable productivity improvement and increased the number of service calls in a day.

ACS also had numerous projects going on during their short construction season. Most teams had from 12 to 16 people and if they needed a part, the entire team often had to wait until the part arrived, and at union rates, the expense for people standing around waiting for parts was substantial. Parts shortages might be caused by warehouse stock outs, mispicks, or delivery errors. The supplier partner who stocked most of the parts used in construction projects agreed to carry additional parts and kit the parts for direct delivery to project sites. The materials didn't touch the ACS warehouse, which had several benefits:

1. Not stocking the parts reduced SKU count, floor space requirements, and warehouse costs.
2. Kitting and direct delivery resulted in more complete shipments with reduced downtime and higher productivity for the construction crews.
3. Project cost tracking was simplified.
4. Time to delivery, if there was an exception, was much shorter, as the supplier could deliver the part directly to the site rather than taking it to the ACS warehouse first.

An unexpected benefit was that more projects were completed during the short construction season.

Recognizing Value in the Partnership

As illustrated in the stories in the preceding text, there is much more value in supplier partnerships than in typical supplier relationships. Cost reductions over time can be much higher than the 3 percent to 6 percent that customers often ask for; in my experience, working in partnership can save as much as 20 percent in materials costs. How does that happen? First, by focusing on a few great suppliers for given commodities, the consolidated purchase volume yields greater discounts and year-end rebates when they apply. Second, having fewer suppliers not only allows for that consolidation, but the indirect costs of invoice processing, check writing, supplier visits, and other supplier management activities are reduced as well.

Relationship pricing can have a dramatic impact on parts costs as well. Relationship pricing involves using annual purchase volumes to establish costs as well as consolidated parts purchases into fewer key supplier partners. If you have two (or at most three) suppliers for given commodities, the consolidation of part numbers and volume purchases can be significant. In addition, having more than one supplier as discussed in Chapter 2 mitigates supply chain risk factors.

The blanket PO can be very effective in relationship management. A blanket PO addresses the quantity of given parts that will be purchased over the long term. It usually covers a year, but the time frame can be longer. Many purchasing professionals don't like using blanket POs because of the misconception that they're a commitment to buying that many parts, but the blanket PO is a planning tool, not a commitment. Suppliers can use them to plan their annual parts flow and production run quantities so that they can reduce costs and pass the savings on to the customer.

The commitment represented by the blanket PO can be whatever the partners agree upon. When I was VP, Operations, we committed to the supplier's lead time for parts. That is, if the supplier's lead time to produce or purchase parts was 30 days, then we committed to buy/protect the parts represented by that lead time. For example, if the blanket PO is for 1,200 parts annually and the lead time is 30 days, our commitment was for 100 parts. We didn't need to receive them all at once by any means. We usually received in Kanban quantities that were much smaller than 100, but if our plans or forecasts changed, we could be on the hook for the 100 parts, thus protecting the supplier. What the supplier did to provide the other 1,100 parts was up to them. If they chose to build in larger batching, thinking that it's cheaper to do so (which it usually isn't), that's up to them. Their goal is to do what they need to do to keep us as a customer, and our goal is to partner with them to get quality parts, just in time at the lowest possible cost.

Supplier partnerships go well beyond cost reduction. Many suppliers have great technical capabilities that can help in product design. The CEO of one metal forming and stamping company had such deep knowledge of metallurgy, he would weigh in during product design on issues such as material choice, heat treating, coating, and tolerances. His knowledge kept our engineers from designing things that couldn't be built effectively and saved his customers many hours of frustration in manufacturing.

In another situation, one company used zinc as a base material in their product. Zinc is traded on the commodities markets, and forward contracts can be purchased during periods of volatile prices that can save a lot of money. Commodities trading can be very risky and your CFO should be part of the team that looks at such approaches, but by working together with supplier partners, you could reach sufficient volumes to set up contracts, when on your own you might not be able to.

International Partnerships

In my role as VP, Operations, our CEO thought all of the VPs should have marketing responsibility. One day he walked into my office and said, "Rick, I finally figured out what you get to do for marketing. You get to open China." And he turned around and walked out. I thought, "Wow, how do I do that?"

We developed a joint venture (JV) agreement with a large Shanghai-based company to manufacture and distribute our products in China. We made access control devices used to access cell tower sites, postboxes, and other applications that recorded the time of entry in remote locations. Getting access to the markets, however, required close contacts with high-level government officials, and our JV partner had such contacts. Many companies try to open business in China with wholly owned subsidiaries, but in our case, having a JV partner was key to our success.

Note that we didn't go to China to try to reduce costs in our U.S. markets. Our inventory turns and service lead times suggested we needed to assemble our products as close to the customer as possible. Add to that the fact that each device was custom coded for the customer and we needed very short supply chains. To open the Chinese market, we needed to manufacture and assemble as much as possible in China to meet government requirements, so we developed the JV.

Partnering with suppliers to provide quality products just in time as close to the customer as possible at the lowest possible cost means using a few, possibly global, supplier partners. Whether they're manufacturers of components or finished goods, shipping companies, third-party logistics (3PL) providers, or producers of unique materials, having partnerships around the world can help extend your core competencies closer to your customer while keeping costs down. Supplier partnerships are second only to customer partnerships (see Chapter 4) in providing high value.

References

Hallion, R.P. Winter. 1990. "A Troubling Past: Air Force Fighter Acquisition Since 1945." *Airpower Journal* 4, no. 4, pp. 4–23.

McChesney, T. "Letter: Fly-off Competitions and Fairness." *Federal Computer Week,* October 22, 2008. Web. August 9, 2016.

CHAPTER 4

How Customer Partnerships Lead to Internal Success

The ultimate partnership is that between suppliers and customers. It is said that the customer defines quality, and in a true customer partnership, customers should be involved in the product design/definition process for all except the most innovative items, so that quality and performance can be properly defined. Many companies either over- or underspecify products because they never asked what the customer needed.

In some cases, customers don't know what they need, and, in that case, innovators should push on but quickly gather feedback for design updates in the second round of release. Apple is very good at this. Steve Jobs often said that customers would have never asked for an iPod, but once they had one they asked for it to be attachable to a shirtsleeve for running and exercise. These feedback loops can dramatically shift the landscape for companies, allowing them to innovate in a responsive way.

Markets change swiftly, and partnerships between suppliers and customers can help address rapid change. Customers need speed—speed in getting products to market, in getting new products from design to distribution, and in responding to unexpected demand. Because markets change so quickly, companies need to be agile and flexible in order to avoid getting caught with obsolete inventory. The ability to shift production and distribution rapidly is a core competency that suppliers need to develop to partner effectively with their customers. By increasing speed, flexibility, and agility, suppliers can dramatically increase their value to their customers.

If you're going to measure only one thing from an operational perspective, it is shipped on time. If you can't ship on time, customers become unhappy and look for new suppliers. By working with customers to help predict and smooth demand, suppliers can serve them better and provide innovative products at the right time in the right quantity at the lowest possible cost.

The concept of the Perfect Order embodies this ideal. A Perfect Order is completely error-free. The measure is of the percentage of orders delivered to the right place with the right product, at the right time, in the right condition, in the right quantity, with the right documentation, and, eventually, with the right invoice. Perfect! Some companies will actually fine their "partners" for errors, sometimes to the tune of many thousands of dollars. Fines are a poor basis for a partnership.

The key here is to align the company's goals with the customer's goals to help everyone serve customers. Once again, collaboration and partnership are different in that regard, much the same as committees and teams. Note that these partnerships apply, no matter what the products or services are; as long as there is a supplier and a customer, partnerships can be developed, even within the company.

By reversing the perspective on the supply chain and looking at the customer first, companies can improve and innovate in ways they never thought of, while optimizing their performance and service levels. After all, your customers have a vested interest in your success.

Can Demand Be Managed?

One of the keys to success in Lean or World Class is smoothing the flow of materials or services throughout the supply chain. One way to accomplish this is by managing demand, which not only improves cash flow and profitability but also allows companies to serve their customers better and allows customers to plan their operations better.

Many companies rely solely on sales forecasts to drive production or distribution planning. They often don't try (or don't know how to use) customer real-time information for planning purposes. Wal-Mart helped pioneer radio frequency identification (RFID) to hasten the flow of product movement information to help plan deliveries and load trucks. Many other companies use point of sale (POS) information to see what products moved from customers' shelves, usually the day before, but sometimes in real time so that shelves can be restocked to maximize sales and service levels.

Toyota uses an allocation process to help their dealers promise very fast turns on cars ordered to customer specifications. Using the allocation process, they tell dealers how many cars of each type they can access and, thus, smooth production at least at the model level. By having very flexible factories, they can produce the options quickly for best customer service.

Partnerships prioritize customer outcomes, rather than profitability and cash flow as driving forces. In her book *Leading With Noble Purpose: How to Create A Tribe of True Believers,* Lisa McLeod writes that when companies focus on their purpose in the context of serving customers first, the profit and cash flow will follow. She cites a number of examples where this perspective led to dramatic growth, far higher than previously achieved with executive focus on profits. In these partnerships, customers are motivated to provide their suppliers with all of the information they need to serve them successfully *and* accelerate profit and growth.

At Supra, we provided our suppliers with a rolling monthly forecast for the next 12 months to help them plan materials and labor flow, thus helping to drive costs down and service levels up. We also had almost 100 percent *Kanban* (an auto replenishment system) with our suppliers, which tended to smooth the flow of materials through smaller, more frequent order quantities. In some cases, every time we submitted a Kanban pull, we also sent an updated short-term forecast to help refine planning, which allowed us to achieve a 99.8 percent shipped on time with inventory turns over 15.

Getting Information Quickly

One of the keys to success in customer partnerships is the rapid movement of information both up and down the supply chain. Remember, partnerships are based on relationship and trust, and the foundation is communication. Getting information and getting it quickly is critical to strong relationships with customers. The kinds of information that can be shared include

- Order information
- Designs

- Product specifications
- Quality requirements
- Invoice/payment information
- Performance measures/scorecards
- General relationship status
- Upcoming needs
- Changes in the way business is being conducted
- Forecasts and plans

The sooner the partners have the information, the sooner they can take action to deliver products and services on time, to specifications, and at the lowest possible cost. Strong, rapid communication helps make that happen.

Customers and suppliers working in partnership can also help design the distribution networks to move materials through the supply chain faster and with lower investment in inventory. Working together to understand product demand and flow, the partners can determine what items should go where to provide the best possible service.

One of my clients was a major distributor of plumbing materials ranging from fire hydrants to sprinkler systems to irrigation systems and construction pipes. They had over 30 branches in the northwestern United States that served a wide variety of customers. Working with their customers to understand the demand and flow of materials in each location, they discovered significant differences in the types of products needed in each region. For instance, demand for irrigation products was high east of the Cascade Mountains, but the population west of the mountains had higher demand for sprinkler systems. Understanding the customers' demand patterns allowed the company to redesign its distribution network for efficient inventory placement while keeping the levels down. This yielded better service, higher profits, and lower capital investment in inventory.

There are a number of ways to foster good communication. Many companies focus on electronic communication, but face-to-face is often the most effective means, especially if the information is complex, important, or proprietary. Many times, using a meeting as an excuse to visit the customer or supplier not only helps cement the relationship but also contextualizes how products and services are used.

One past client made metal parts for military vehicles that were produced by the customer. We asked the customer to bring a completed truck to my client's facility so that the employees who made the parts could see how they were used on the truck. The employees enjoyed climbing around on the truck looking for the parts they had made, and when they saw their parts, it was like a proud papa looking at his baby in the nursery. The perspective that provided made a difference to the employees' attention to detail and understanding of performance, which made the quality and speed of delivery even better.

Having meetings alternating between customer and supplier locations helps in many ways. At Supra, our purchasing team visited key suppliers every six months and the suppliers visited us on alternate quarters. That way, we could see how the suppliers were making our parts and they could see how their parts were used. In addition, many more people could be involved in meetings and tours, further solidifying the relationships. As VP, Operations, I'd go along on the visits at least once a year to build my relationships with the executives of the supplier company, which was particularly useful when something happened that needed executive intervention, such as reallocation of resources to meet a crisis or opportunity.

Tools such as e-mail and video conferencing can be effective for certain kinds of communication, but I feel strongly that nothing beats face-to-face for strengthening relationships. A good mix of frequent communication can provide dividends when working with partners.

Thinking Backward: Reverse the Supply Chain for Innovative Results

Many companies think about how their suppliers can better serve them through services such as vendor-managed inventory (VMI), where the supplier comes onsite, inspects the inventory-holding locations to see if replenishment is needed, and delivers and stocks the product without anyone from the company actually touching the stock. This saves a lot of labor time and provides just-in-time delivery, which can dramatically reduce inventory levels and invested cash. The interesting thing is that companies can do that for their customers as well, but often they don't think about proposing it as a service until the customer asks. Most companies should just turn around and look down the supply chain toward their customer and provide the same services to them that they ask for from their suppliers.

One innovative approach is to improve customer service levels by having the customers run your warehouse operations. Alaska Communications (ACS) dramatically cut warehouse costs and increased service to its construction contractor customers by having the contractors actually run the company's warehouses. ACS provides wire line services throughout the state of Alaska. Each year, it tackles major construction projects to install and maintain telecommunications infrastructure. To provide better service to customers and construction crews, the company has several warehouses throughout the state, two of which experienced highly variable demand but were staffed full-time.

ACS partnered with a contractor to replace ACS warehouse personnel with part-time contractor personnel to create a variable workforce (in balance with variable demand) and improve service. The contractor provided personnel as needed to receive and dispense materials at the warehouses to construction crews at (potentially) all hours of the day.

The result was a win for both parties. ACS reduced their labor costs by 75 percent and gained much-needed flexibility to handle the highly variable load during the construction season. Outsourcing improved service levels, reduced costs, improved agility, and boosted capacity. ACS avoided layoffs by not replacing staff members who retired.

The customers reaped several benefits from the new arrangement, including better communications with ACS, early notification of new project opportunities, and flexible hours for the warehouse location that better met their needs. This partnership between ACS and its contractor/customer had its rough spots initially, but trust, relationship, and strong communication helped both companies increase their capacity and profitability beyond what they could have achieved separately.

Auto replenishment systems such as Kanban and VMI can help manage and smooth demand to shorten supply chains and accelerate the movement of materials. This not only helps improve service but also allows new products and designs to be introduced more quickly and without exposure to slow and obsolete inventory.

Using Supplier-Managed Delivery to Improve Customer Service

ACS has a unique challenge being in the state of Alaska where winter lasts almost eight months a year. For a telecom company, putting fiber cable into the ground, building small support buildings throughout the state, and putting up communications towers can be particularly challenging when the ground is frozen. A typical construction team, the internal customer for supply chain management, is comprised of 12 to 16 people and the projects can be miles away from any support such as motels and restaurants. Sometimes movement has to occur using snow-cats, snowmobiles, and other nontraditional means. Suffice it to say that if crews are standing around waiting for parts, the costs can add up very quickly.

ACS used to do almost all of their own kitting and delivery of parts from central or branch warehouses strategically located around the state. Parts requirements would be planned by construction engineering, ordered by purchasing, and stored in the warehouses until needed by the construction project. Some of the difficulties in delivery of complete parts kits included

- Lead times from suppliers
- One project "borrowing" parts allocated to another project
- Warehouse mispicks
- Warehouse out-of-stock situations
- Lack of standardized parts callouts

All too often, crews had to wait for parts before they could complete their jobs.

The company decided to partner with one of their key suppliers to have the supplier kit the entire construction package at the supplier's warehouse and deliver the kit directly to the construction site, or place the kit in a container, which could be delivered to ACS and transshipped to the site without being opened. The supplier would even arrange for parts they didn't normally carry to complete the kit for shipment.

The results of this partnership included

- Dramatic reduction of parts shortages and waiting at the construction locations
- Construction jobs being completed quicker, allowing for more jobs to be done during the short construction season
- Inventory at the warehouses was cut by almost 75 percent
- Warehouse activity was reduced and productivity greatly improved

There were also great benefits for the supplier partner:

- Increased volume of business because they provided the total span of parts for all jobs
- The ability to leverage their warehouse resources due to the increased volumes for greater productivity and use of assets
- "Locking in" the business by becoming the key supplier for construction projects
- Better pricing from their own suppliers because they were buying in larger volume
- A seat on the project design team so that they could see requirements much earlier, allowing better plannings

This became a big win for both partners and served the internal customer (the construction teams) much more effectively.

ACS also achieved dramatic results by developing creative ways to partner with external customers. Their Juneau warehouse was only open from 8:00 a.m. to 5:00 p.m. five days a week, due to the total annual volume of activity, but during the summer construction season, it is light outside for over 20 hours a day. Contractors liked to maximize their activities during those long daylight periods and were frustrated that the warehouse was not available during the entire daylight period. Rather than add staff for the short construction season, which was difficult due to both limited availability of people and training requirements, ACS approached the customer/contractors and asked if they would be interested in running the warehouse for ACS during the summer. One contractor jumped at the chance.

One concern was ACS's ability to control parts when they were essentially letting the fox into the henhouse. But since ACS brought all of the parts to the warehouse from suppliers in Seattle or by transfer from other warehouses, they knew exactly what was going to the Juneau location. Because ACS provided the specifications for the construction projects, they knew exactly what should be going out, and periodic audits checked what remained in the warehouse. The operating contractor owned any discrepancies.

The result was a 65 percent reduction in warehouse costs for ACS and much greater project productivity for the contractor. The contractor also had the advantage of seeing the parts arrive for new projects far sooner than when they used to be notified. This customer partnership provided dramatic benefits to both parties in the relationship.

CHAPTER 5

Working in the Community

A partnership that many companies overlook is that with their local community. Sustainability, labor force availability, offshoring, reshoring, and job creation are all vital for strong companies and strong communities. In today's world, the lack of skilled workers prevents many companies from growing to the level they desire. This chapter shows how they can partner with the academic community, local government, and not-for-profits to accelerate growth and profitability.

Social Responsibility for Partnerships

Many companies today are finding it increasingly difficult to find workers, particularly at the skilled levels of the organization; welders, machine operators, maintenance mechanics, technical assembly, and many other skills are getting harder to find. Many K-12 school systems focus on college as a follow-on, and many of the trade and vocational programs of the past are disappearing. But there are ways to create public/private partnerships between businesses and universities and especially community colleges to help fulfill the need for skilled workers.[1]

Starting at a basic level, one option for companies is the professional skills training program provided by community colleges to help train and place injured workers. Vocational rehab counselors design these programs to help injured workers develop a path to employment and support local companies' needs. The program operates in three-moth segments for up to a year with training and an internship. There is little or no cost to the employer because the program covers training costs, internship payments, and any additional needed courses. There is even a small payment to the employer to cover some of the time spent managing the

---

[1] Wright (2008).

worker's internship. The employer is expected to seriously consider hiring the worker at the end of the internship, assuming the worker meets the company's needs. These programs provide wins for both the worker and the employer in concert with the community college and professional counselors. A win, win, win, win relationship.

Another option is for companies to work with sheltered workshops and organizations that help people with disabilities find jobs and develop a sense of independence and inclusion in society. Tillamook Country Smoker (TCS) is one story of how successful this kind of partnership can be.

Tillamook is a small town on the Oregon coast at the base of the rain forests of the Coast Range. Three industries support Tillamook: fishing, forest products, and dairy farming and associated products such as cheese. The area tends to support families in lower- and middle-income ranges. Life is quiet and people support each other in the close-knit community.

TCS began in the 1960s as a small meat market owned by the Crossleys and the Waltzes. The business was seasonal because Tillamook winters are gray and rainy, and activity is slow. The problem with a meat store is what to do with the chicken, beef, and pork in those slow winter months. The families decided to smoke it and make jerky and snack sticks such as pepperoni, which allowed the store to survive. Their reputation for making tasty meat snacks began to grow, and in the mid-1970s, the Smith family approached the Crossleys to build the business with more sales and marketing. Turned down by several banks for loans, the company sought investment and the Ginger family provided loans so that the company could grow the smoker business. Today, TCS has about 300 employees and distributes meat snacks all over the United States and internationally.

The company recognizes that the community has supported it through its initial lean years and through the past 30 years of steady growth. The city helped the company with its building projects and other permitting. The three owner families (by this time, the Waltzes had left the business) decided that they should give something back to their community. One way they did that was by partnering with the Marie Mills Center in Tillamook, a nonprofit that serves the intellectually and developmentally disabled.

Every day, a team of 8 to 15 people from the Marie Mills Center and their supervisors come to work on a bus. They support packaging activities such as bundling bags used for pepperoni sticks, putting lids on jars, and filling packages on the "chew" production line, a ground jerky snack. They work a full shift, take breaks and lunch, and are very reliable workers.

The company could easily automate everything they do, but management says it feels good to give these people meaning in their lives. Their pay allows them to go to the stores in Tillamook to shop and participate in society in ways they wouldn't otherwise be able to. They have a sense of pride in their work. Dick Crossley, the COO, says that the workers from the Marie Mills Center love their work, and whenever he walks through the area, the smiles and hugs he receives are the highlight of his day.

The work also helps the individuals overcome some mental and health-related issues. One worker on the team used to have over 100 seizures a day, which were so severe she had to wear a helmet to protect herself. Now with the work she is doing for TCS, she has as few as one seizure per day. She gives Dick some of the biggest hugs he gets.

The company also benefits from this partnership because the labor force in Tillamook is limited and with the growth they have achieved, finding good workers is difficult. This reliable resource helps reduce the company's staffing worries.

This is a perfect example of a community partnership that benefits the company, the individuals, and the community. The company has chosen to give back, even though they could have taken a different approach through automation, the workers achieve a richer life, and the community benefits economically. This partnership is truly a win/win/win.

Creating Jobs While Reducing Labor

Many companies are finding ways to create jobs while reducing labor. I know that sounds counterintuitive, but all you need to look at is the cost of labor as a percentage of sales. If you can reduce the overall percentage while adding jobs over time, you can create or at least save jobs for the local community. At Supra, when we were at $13 million in sales, labor was 13 percent of sales. By the time we got to almost $60 million in sales, labor was only 3 percent of sales. At the same time, we had not laid anyone off. We started with 61 people in production and ended with 62 people in production. They also earned more per hour and had much better benefits than before.

By focusing on productivity, companies can provide a strong job environment for the community and become an employer of choice, which makes it easier to find staff when needed. Many companies (and economists, for that matter) measure productivity as output per hour, but that doesn't allow for cheap hours or expensive hours. I believe that Jack Welch was right when he said productivity is measured as units of output per unit of input. I believe those units need to be the same: dollars of output per dollar of input. So, what is the revenue dollar value of output per cost dollar of input? For labor, it is total direct labor cost divided by revenue.

Many accountants believe labor is a variable cost, that is, it varies directly with revenue. However, that isn't actually true because in the short run, most companies don't lay people off week by week because it's too difficult to get trained workers back again when business picks up. Therefore, labor should be treated as a fixed cost in the short run, and variability should be managed through temporary workers or overtime, the only truly variable labor costs.

Given that the real economic driver of a company is output, activity measures such as building inventory don't provide real value and shouldn't be considered in meaningful measures of output. Labor and materials should always be measured as a function of revenue.

If companies had used those types of measures as well as consideration of total cost of ownership (TCO), many of the offshoring initiatives we saw in the 1980s wouldn't have happened. Through productivity initiatives such as World Class Manufacturing, Six Sigma, and, eventually, Lean, companies could have achieved labor productivity rates that would have precluded moving production to low-cost countries. Productivity in the United States is often assessed at 10 times that of low-cost countries, making the effective labor rate close to, if not cheaper than, low-cost countries. The delays and other issues associated with offshore supply more than outweighed those costs, which we discuss in the next section.

If companies asked, "How can we keep jobs while improving profitability?" they may have discovered that with dramatic productivity improvement such as that provided by the Toyota Production System, they could have kept jobs in the United States and still accelerated profit and growth. Unfortunately, the cost-accounting systems used at the time did not provide the holistic information needed to make partnership decisions.

Reshoring and Keeping Jobs Local

Many companies are considering whether and how to reshore manufacturing as a way to support corporate objectives and bring jobs back to the United States. Many companies, both large and small, are looking at reshoring because of its benefits for competitiveness. In 2014, for the first time in two decades, the United States realized a net gain in jobs when comparing reshoring to offshoring.[2] But the real key to deciding where to produce isn't just the patriotic or political goal of creating jobs in the United States.

The original trend toward offshoring started in the early 1990s with major movement of production into the Far East, particularly China.[3] While imported products have long come from Japan, Taiwan, and other Eastern countries, moving manufacturing plants to low-cost countries such as China gained momentum due to low labor costs in those countries. Many companies saw the opportunity to increase margins and profits by doing so, often without considering issues like different time zones, inventory costs, quality, and intellectual property protection.

As labor costs in the Far East increased and companies focused more on being close to their customers, some have brought production back to the United States, which focused academic attention on onshore manufacturing, yielding studies on its benefits. Soon the tide began to shift, and more companies "came back" and were glad they did.

Why did companies originally decide to go offshore? The obvious reason was the very low cost of labor. When offshoring first started, Chinese labor rates were a fraction of those in the United States. The standard costing systems used by many companies showed that it was

---

[2] Regole (2015).
[3] Pay (2011).

much cheaper to produce offshore and bring products into the United States than to produce in the United States. In some cases, companies had other reasons to go offshore such as

- Access to technology
- Lower materials cost
- Access to the newly opening Chinese markets
- Proximity to other Far Eastern markets
- Low transportation cost

However, in many cases, companies soon experienced challenges related to offshoring such as

- Communication problems
  - o Language
  - o Time zone differences
- Unreliable supply
  - o Quality issues
  - o Delivery reliability
- Increasing costs
  - o Labor
  - o Transportation
  - o Exchange rates and the favorable U.S. dollar

In addition, small- and middle-market companies were soon left behind as the Chinese in particular discovered that working with larger U.S. companies had many benefits in terms of product volume, use of technology, intellectual property that could be copied, and more. The better producers soon turned their attention to larger U.S. companies, leaving small companies to fend for themselves with smaller, less reliable producers. Companies then began to realize how important it was to consider TCO when deciding to change location.

TCO includes three groupings of cost considerations:

1. Pretransaction costs
2. Transaction costs
3. Posttransaction costs

Pretransaction costs include

- Engineering and design
- Materials requirements
- Supplier sourcing
- Travel costs related to engineering and production start-up
- Contracting and local legal understanding
- Adapting IT systems
- Developing ordering processes

Transaction costs include

- Item price
- Order placement costs
- Pipeline costs such as
  o Transportation
  o Customs
  o Inventory costs
  o Freight damage and loss
- Receiving costs
- Quality inspection
- Return of parts
- Scrap
- Resolving order-related issues
- Payment
- Special regulatory requirements such as insect control and pallet type

Posttransaction costs include

- Quality issues on local assembly lines
- Defect and reject resolution
- Field failures and warranty
- Repair parts
- Cost of materials and packaging disposal
- Obsolescence driven by larger order sizes

- Handling of shipping containers
- Cost of holding inventory driven by order size

Most cost accounting systems don't consider these "product" costs, and many companies didn't consider them when deciding whether or not to offshore production. Unfortunately, once they started rearing their ugly heads, companies learned that distance matters in supply chain management, and the tide began to turn.

The equation for TCO is

$$TCO = A + PV (O + T + M + I + E - S)$$

A = acquisition cost
PV = present value
O = operating costs
T = training costs
M = maintenance costs
I = inventory costs
E = environmental costs
S = salvage value

This is not to say that all offshoring is bad, even though it moves jobs overseas. If your customers are in the Far East, it makes sense both from a cost and service perspective to move some production offshore to be near your customers, shorten your supply chains, and reduce costs. But before you do that, it is incumbent on your supply chain and product development teams to look at the larger picture of where production should be relative to your product development department and your customers. It is particularly interesting to me that Chinese companies see the logic of this and buy U.S.-based producers to gain access to U.S. markets, intellectual property, and suppliers. Developing a supply chain strategy that takes all of this into account allows companies to make well-informed decisions and to partner with the community to maintain or bring back jobs to the United States.

This is not just a one-way street where companies do all of the heavy lifting to benefit their communities. Communities can help companies remain in the United States as well. Cities and counties need to look at the regulations and taxes they place on companies, which are part of the cost model used to choose locations. Many communities provide tax abatement to entice companies to locate there. South Carolina, in particular, has open doors for companies to move there, as shown by Boeing and BMW. Other communities offer skills training programs to help provide the skilled workers that companies need. Infrastructure spending also has an impact.

Once I was working with a company that made pet furniture to decide where to place a distribution center to serve Eastern U.S. customers. Cat furniture—scratching posts, "cat condos," climbing ramps, beds, and so on—is a billion dollar business. My client needed to shorten their supply chains to help their customers with just-in-time product delivery so that retailers could minimize inventory and maximize service levels to customers. A distribution center in the East was a requirement.

As we began to explore locations, the first consideration was the transportation system in the East. The Appalachian Mountains run through the eastern states and the freeway system is on the east or west side of those mountains with just a few crossings. Trucking is the primary mode of transportation for cat furniture and we had to pick a location with easy freeway access that allowed us to deliver our product to our customers' main distribution centers.

Then we had to look at the availability of low-skilled labor. It turns out that there are a number of military bases where spouses were looking for jobs. Finally, we needed to consider the government environment including jobs programs, tax abatements, and so on. We ended up selecting a location outside of Cincinnati that kept our supply chains short, reduced costs, and provided excellent service levels to the customers. If we had simply looked at distance to customers or low-cost labor, we would not have selected the location we did.

Community partnerships, including using sheltered workshops, developing training programs, easing the process of building new plants or warehouses, and employing people in the United States, all provide great benefit to companies and their communities. Public/private partnerships drive accelerated profit and growth for companies, which in turn benefits their communities. Strong partnerships like these are worth the time they take to develop.

References

Pay, R. 2011. *Re-shoring: Bringing Business Back Home*, Operationspayoff.com. May 10.

Regole, R. 2015. "The Drivers of Manufacturing Reshoring." *Industry Week*, July 23.

Wright, R. Spring 2008. "How to Get the Most From University Relationships." *MIT Sloan Management Review*, pp. 75–80.

CHAPTER 6

How to Tell Your Partner They're Screwing Up

Two keys to strong partnerships are (1) knowing what is expected, and (2) knowing how you're measuring up to those expectations. Whether your partnerships are internal or external, feedback is important to building strong relationships. In addition, feedback needs to be a two-way street where both sides measure the other's performance. I've seen far too many situations where one party thought everything was fine, while the other party was ready to jump ship.

Why Measure Performance?

Measures help communicate what is important and whether those objectives are being met or exceeded. When partners know the score, they can push for improvements that benefit everyone, which continues to build trust and communication, the foundation for strong partnerships.

Most people like to be part of a winning team, and to know if they are winning, it helps to know the score. For employees, knowing how they're performing not only helps them improve, but it also removes the stress of uncertainty. If things aren't good, they usually know either how to correct the situation or that management needs to provide guidance. When companies openly communicate their overall performance score to employees, they can reduce turnover by squelching any rumors that might drive turnover and, in many cases, can avoid unionization.

The same is true with suppliers. If they know how they're performing, they can make improvements that could reduce costs, improve delivery performance and quality, and potentially increase their revenue and profitability as well.

Knowing What's Important: Setting Objectives

Any partnership, whether internal or external, has to have objectives that are common to both parties. For instance, if the partnership is between operations and sales, meeting the promises made to the customer has to be important to both parties. Coming together to achieve the objective creates a solid relationship, like a husband and wife who both want to raise the kids well and thus share the load, perhaps doing different things that help achieve the overall objective.

As discussed in Chapter 2, the memo of understanding with your suppliers does just that. It clarifies the objectives and how each side is expected to contribute. For suppliers, the three key performance criteria are usually quality, delivery, and cost reduction (we're looking for cost improvement, not necessarily the lowest possible cost). For operation partnerships with engineering, the key criteria might be meeting/exceeding the customer's needs, designing a product that can be manufactured at a reasonable cost and lead time, and making sure the products can be successfully transitioned into production. For partnerships with accounting, criteria might be timely and accurate reporting, assistance in understanding and resolving issues with the financial statements, and strong metrics for accountability.

Setting expectations happens at the beginning of the relationship. For an employee, expectations might be listed in an employment agreement or the employee handbook. For suppliers, a certification process during the qualification phase may lay out and measure the supplier's key attributes, which will be reassessed regularly. The objectives for the relationship might include

- Reduce costs
- Increase quality
- Improve customer service
- Raise operating efficiency
- Lower total inventories
- Eliminate/minimize inspections
- Eliminate scrap and rework

If partners are measuring different things or one side isn't measuring anything at all, the relationship is out of balance; one partner thinks it is doing just fine while the other partner is worried. For example, a client company produced a medical supply item and thought their shipped on time was about 60 percent, which is not good. Several important customers were starting to look elsewhere for supply. When I went in, I found that my client was measuring shipped on time based on order line items. Using this system, if there were 10 items on the order and 9 were shipped on time, their score was 90 percent. However, the customer was unhappy because one of the items was late. Because each side measured shipped on time differently, they were not seeing eye to eye, and the company was at risk of losing valuable customers.

At another company, the order line items were part of a residential lawn sprinkler system. If one item was missing, even if it was a low-cost and seemingly less important "C" item, the system as a whole could not be installed. My client found that when they had a shortage, the installer often went to the competitor for the entire system, not just the one missing part. The client did not measure order fulfillment and they certainly did not measure lost sales. It turns out they could have increased revenues by 5 percent to 10 percent by simply performing better, but first they had to realize they had a problem.

My philosophy of shipped on time was that either the order was shipped complete and on time, or it was a complete miss. At the medical supply company, when we measured shipped on time on that basis, we discovered it was a dismal 24 percent. No wonder the customers were so unhappy. As it turned out, the VP, Operations, knew that the shipping performance was that bad, and he sandbagged the numbers. When that came to light, the CEO fired him. Amazingly enough, when we began measuring shipped on time properly, the problem became obvious and within a month, the real performance moved to 80 percent and eventually to 98 percent. Many times, people simply need to know what the real score is in order to improve it.

What Measurements Accomplish

Measurements are intended to improve performance and change behaviors. Other than supplier scorecards, most measures are internal and many are based on the financial reporting system. However, a set of objectives between partners should have defined measures so that both parties know if the objectives are being met. The objectives should be the business outcomes that benefit both partners. It is important to develop measures that look at both historical perspectives and forward helping to predict the future. There are two reasons to start measuring as soon as possible in the relationship:

1. Often the biggest improvement happens at the beginning of the relationship.
2. When people see that the relationship is working early on, they're motivated to continue, which helps overcome doubt and inertia.

Many measures are designed as the gauges of a process, telling people if the process is under control and producing the expected results. Other measures are designed to improve productivity and hold people accountable for results.

The best measures reinforce discipline in the organization, which requires well-defined systems and processes. Then measures reinforce behavior and accountability, which promotes adherence to the rules of the systems and processes (see Figure 6.1). Overall, strong operations discipline leads to an environment of continuous improvement, which fosters evolutionary change over time.

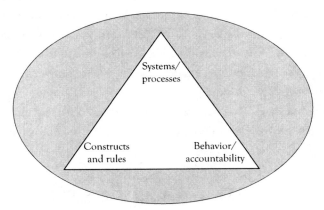

Figure 6.1 Operations discipline

What Gets Measured Gets Managed

"What gets measured gets managed" is the watchword in partnerships. By letting people know the score, behaviors change, and performance and communication improve. Over the years, I've seen many suppliers react with great surprise when we presented them with a scorecard of their performance. They thought they were doing fine when we thought they were one of the worst suppliers we had. Agreeing on how performance will be measured is a key item in the memo of understanding that serves as the foundation of the relationship.

There are four areas of measurement that are important for suppliers:

1. Quality
2. Delivery
3. Cost reduction
4. Customer service and responsiveness

Quality measures should be a function of the total failures, both incoming and in-house (as used), as a percent of the total parts received. Delivery should be a function of late (or exceptionally early) items as a percent of total received, to calculate an on-time percentage. Cost reduction is a function of the total cost reductions the supplier has suggested. Customer service and responsiveness, an often overlooked measure, can be a function of how easy the supplier is to deal with on invoice problems, late orders, emergency situations, shipping/packaging quality, and so on. Often, the input for these measures may come from other departments in your organization such as accounting. Not only should the raw scores in each area be traced and reported, but also the trend should be monitored and reported to show whether improvement is occurring.

The Supplier Self-Inspection Program is a great way to measure supplier performance. Its goal is to assure the customers that the product would pass an incoming inspection. Again, it is critical that the measures be the same on both sides as laid out in the inspection requirements so that both parties measure the same way. Then if the supplier has a certified measuring process, the customer does not need to do an incoming inspection at all. Simply tracking field failures and on-line failures will tell you whether the supplier should remain certified or not. If so, the receiving party doesn't need to do further inspections, saving time and expense. The ultimate supplier partner is one that meets expectations on all of the performance criteria including a self-inspection program.

A program of supplier reviews and audits can boost your supplier partners' performance over the long term. Your company should conduct face-to-face meetings with key suppliers three to four times per year. It is best to alternate the location between your facility and theirs so that both parties can see how the other operates. During these meetings, you should review

- Monthly performance reports
- Performance as measured by the on-site audit
- Any new product development or changes that impact the supplier
- Forecast performance and changes
- Action plans to increase the value provided by the supplier
- The elements of total cost of ownership (TCO) and elimination of waste
- The status of the overall relationship

It is useful to have company executives sit in on a couple of these visits each year to help develop the relationship at the top. Those relationships can be useful if there are ever problems that require higher-level intervention.

Measures can drive performance improvements in many kinds of relationships. In my job as VP, Operations, we used sales forecasts as part of our operations and supply chain process. For years, we had tried to get more accurate forecasts from sales, but they did not see the value in providing them; so when they did, they were often highly inaccurate to ensure that they could meet or beat their numbers. Then one of my managers came up with an idea: create a competition among the salespeople to provide better forecasts and reward the winner each month with lunch. I doubted that a lunch by itself would drive change to the degree we needed, so we decided to post the results each month in the lunchroom.

By using peer pressure and tapping into salespeople's competitive nature, the forecasts became more accurate very quickly. The measure was simply actual as a percent of forecast, and the person closest to 100 percent won. We measured that way because a low miss and a high miss were both just as bad. We knew we would not get to perfection since accurate forecasting is an oxymoron, but we got much more useful forecasts than before.

Another thing we measured internally was the number of days from month end to publication of the financial statements, which at many companies takes 20 to 30 days. Our CFO drove improvement to the point that the accounting department published the financial statements four days after month end. Even though financial results are backward-looking measures, getting them promptly helped the VPs and managers improve performance throughout the company. Then, combined with other changes in our cost-accounting system, we could access our performance results weekly or even on demand. I had daily information on shipments and weekly data on overtime, scrap percentages, supplier performance, and whether suppliers were missing their due dates. In many cases, all I had to do was walk around and review the scoreboards in each department to get a sense of how things were going. This allowed us to make changes well before month end to correct any issues.

Sample Measures for Internal Scorecard—Higher Level

- Executive level
  - Revenue growth
  - Profit growth
  - Cash flow
- Sales
  - Sales to plan
  - Percent of sales from new customers
  - Cost of sales as percent of total sales
  - Accounts receivable days
  - Customer accommodations
- Operations/supply chain
  - Order lead time
  - Shipped on time/perfect order
  - Labor as a percent of sales

- o Inventory days
- o Warranty as a percent of sales
- • Design engineering
  - o Revenue from new products
  - o Days to first revenue from new products
  - o Products successfully transitioned into production
  - o Projects completed on time and on budget
- • Accounting
  - o Number of days to close
  - o Accounts payable days

Most measures should be tracked over time so that you know if things are getting better or worse, especially if you have a continuous improvement culture in your organization. All of our key measures were displayed with a trend line showing change. It is important that the measure be calculated so that an upward trend line shows improvement. Psychologically, people understand that lines that go up are good and lines that go down are bad.

The chart in Figure 6.2 shows how materials cost is performing. Since materials costs are almost always variable, it is important to measure them as a function of sales/revenue. As sales increase, one would expect materials cost to increase in real dollars as well, but is it increasing as a percent of sales (which is bad)? Since there is the potential for product mix to influence that, the timeline should be relatively long. Most of the items above the gross profit line such as materials, labor, cost of sales, commissions,

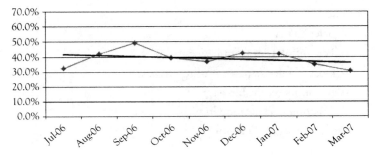

Figure 6.2 Material % trend

and warranty (your variable costs) should be measured as a percentage of sales, not as a raw number. For instance, if labor this month was $500,000 and last month it was $450,000, is that bad? You really don't know until you know what shipments were and how much labor should have been spent to make those shipments. If sales last month was $4,000,000 and sales this month is $5,000,000, the $500,000 labor number is actually better (11.3 percent vs. 10 percent).

The chart in Figure 6.3 shows the performance of a fixed cost element, operating expenses. Because those costs are not relative to sales, an uptrend is bad, as indicated by the upward arrow. In this chart, the trend line is going up, which is also bad. Without the trend line, it would be hard to tell in this case whether things are getting better or worse, but the trend line makes it very clear.

For items below the gross profit line, comparison should always be made to budget. The items below the line should be largely fixed costs and they should meet expectations based on company size and performance to plan (budget). For example, if the administrative function is designed to cost $600,000 for a $50,000,000 company, then monthly comparisons should look at budget versus actual spend, considering a planned cost of $50,000 per month.

Employees should also know how the company is performing. Many middle-market company owners are afraid to reveal the company's financial performance to the employees out of fear that if the company is making too much money, employees will expect raises or that if

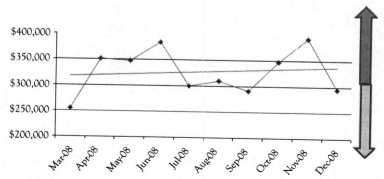

Figure 6.3 Operating expense

performance is poor, employees will leave. Over the years, I've found that employees appreciate the openness, and they expect the company and its owners to make money. Many people, even at the lower levels in the organization, understand risk and reward and feel that the owners deserve a reasonable level of reward. If you try to hide that performance, trust evaporates. It benefits the company as a whole to share basic sales, costs, and profit before tax with your employees.

CHAPTER 7

Getting Close to Engineers

Developing partnerships between design engineering, sales, and operations can drive a level of competitive advantage that dramatically increases the company's overall performance. The process of developing new products and supporting existing product portfolios is vital to the company's strategic positioning. Unfortunately, many companies leave this to marketing or design engineering, who then "throw it over the wall" to sales and production, often leading to weak sales, high costs, long lead times, and other factors that adversely impact the company's performance.

Operations Is From Mars, Engineering Is From Venus

The main focus of operations is to ship the product on time, with customer-defined quality at the lowest possible cost. In many companies, operations includes supply chain, so the process of acquiring materials falls under the control of operations. In other companies, supply chain (or perhaps just purchasing) is separate, making the process a bit more complex and often creating counteracting priorities.

I once worked at a company where purchasing reported to the VP, Operations, and where materials shortages were usually blamed on either lack of forecasts from sales or lack of production plans and requirements from manufacturing. I changed the reporting relationship so that each production manager had his or her own materials team, and amazingly, the materials shortages stopped. I also made the production managers responsible for work-in-process inventory so that the levels remained low. We still had a materials manager so that the policies and processes used to manage materials acquisition and flow were consistent throughout the company.

Engineering's main focus is to design products that can be success-ful in the marketplace and give the company a technological advantage. Often, engineers will use the latest technology and design products in a vacuum to maximize performance, often without regard for the impact on materials and production. This can result in significant increases in SKUs (stock-keeping units or part numbers), high variation in the assem-bly of products, and unnecessary costs.

At the company where I was VP, Operations, we made access con-trol lockboxes that had a pouch for the key used to unlock a house. The pouch design included four screws designed specifically for this applica-tion, which cost $0.16 each. That was $0.64 per lockbox, and with over 300,000 lockboxes produced in a year, that brought the cost of just those four screws to almost $200,000 annually. Not only did they require a special screwdriver because of the design of the head, but also there was only one source. By redesigning the pouch to use standard screws, we reduced the costs to less than 10 percent of the original. Then we looked at a more substantial redesign to eliminate the fasteners entirely.

Developing partnerships between engineering and operations allows for effectively making trade-offs between

- Product cost
- Design capabilities
- Quality
- Production flexibility
- Supplier capabilities
- Time to market

By focusing on their mutual and company-level objectives, engineer-ing and operations together can help the company be more successful and more competitive in the marketplace.

Cleaning Out the Garage

The first step in any process improvement activity is to eliminate anything that's not necessary and the second step is to simplify. When engineering and operations are working in partnership, these two key steps will be the same. Eliminating duplicate parts, unnecessary parts, and duplicate suppliers can yield much simpler designs and form a strong basis for design for manufacturability/design for assembly (DFM/DFA) and design for supply chain management (DFSCM).

Helping engineering set up their own inventory of items for testing and product development can ease the process of managing inventory and keeping it accurate. At Supra, engineers often visited the warehouse to "borrow" inventory to use in their design and testing projects. They would wander through the warehouse, select what they needed, and take it to their workstations. Of course, those items rarely came back. Since the engineers were in a hurry and weren't familiar with the inventory transaction processes in the warehouse, the use of those items was never recorded, which created small but significant inventory variances. Supra was on a just-in-time inventory management system with inventory turns in the vicinity of 17 times. Missing even a few parts could cause problems in production.

The warehouse people set up a separate area with shelves and cabinets containing a selection of parts just for the engineers. The parts on those shelves were transacted to development accounts and expensed, and the engineers could come and take whatever they wanted, whenever they wanted. If they needed something that wasn't in the cabinets, they went to the warehouse manager to get what they needed, which actually made the engineers happy, because they didn't need to wander around the warehouse looking for what they needed.

At Alaska Communications (ACS), we conducted a brief study to find out how many duplicate parts lurked in the warehouses throughout Alaska. It turned out that when engineers developed the components lists for a construction project, they usually used parts they were familiar with rather than selecting from a list maintained by the supply chain staff, which resulted in as many as seven different SKUs for the same item. It also meant there were more suppliers than necessary, which created more work for the purchasing department that bought the parts, and the accounting department, which paid for them. By working with engineering to consolidate the "authorized" parts for construction projects, we cut the number of SKUs in the warehouse by about 50 percent. This also offered a cost reduction opportunity, as purchase volumes increased, allowing the company to save money on the parts through volume discounts. ACS then went through the warehouse and consolidated all of the old parts into an area where they could be

1. Retuned to suppliers for credit
2. Used until gone
3. Sold to other companies
4. Used for other purposes
5. Given to employees at cost or less
6. Recycled
7. Thrown away

Twelve dumpsters of old materials were removed from the main warehouse. This allowed substantial savings in space, which was repurposed.

Working Together to Improve Designs

The concepts of DFM/DFA and DFSCM were developed in an attempt to overcome these sorts of issues. In the 1980s and 1990s, a process called concurrent engineering expanded the design team to include representatives from production, purchasing, and even suppliers in an attempt to optimize designs for manufacturability and bridge the chasm between engineering and operations. The goals were to simplify design, minimize the number of parts, and optimize the production processes needed to assemble the final product. Later, there was also an effort to optimize the design, so that the unit could be repaired or refurbished, and reduce the lifetime cost for the customer by allowing parts to be easily replaced.

Balancing the needs of the product portfolio with controlling the extent of product mix is important in order to manage the breadth of parts, suppliers, production processes, and skills necessary to meet customer needs. By working together, engineering and operations can develop new production technology and capabilities, balancing them with current capabilities to control costs, capacity, and technology in production and distribution.

To help cross the chasm, Hewlett Packard developed a policy where design engineers actually followed their designed products into production and supported them for about six months, when they could then return to design engineering to design additional products. Of course, most design engineers prefer design-to-production support, so this encouraged better designs and the transition could happen faster. As side benefits, this improved customer service and reduced costs.

In many companies, the manufacturing engineering or process engineering functions report to design engineering. That is because those functions help design the processes that need to be put in place to produce, package, and distribute products, and it makes sense, at least initially, to assign them to the design team. The problem with that organization design is that the design team's objectives come first, and often the needs of production and distribution are lower on the ladder of importance. Companies should consider moving process and packaging engineering as close to the activity as possible, while still actively including them in the design process. By having manufacturing/process engineers report to operations, not only is DFM/DFA more effective, but during periods of decreased design activity, they can assist with Lean and other continuous improvement activities.

Manufacturing engineers are key members of the supplier selection and management team as well. They can be active in developing, measuring, and helping to manage supplier partners. In some companies, manufacturing engineers will spend up to half their time at supplier sites, measuring process capabilities, solving quality issues, reducing costs (savings are shared), and generally strengthening the supplier partnerships described in Chapters 2 and 3.

Ramp-Up/Ramp-Down

The product development life cycle (Figure 7.1) is a familiar concept to almost everyone involved in production and distribution. The four-stage life cycle is one that every company should consider as they manage their product portfolio.

Unfortunately, in the excitement of new product development, many companies will make great effort in managing the first two stages and then skim over the last two, especially the decline stage. Bringing in numerous new products without getting rid of old ones causes the

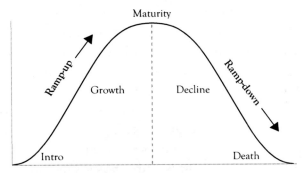

Figure 7.1 Product life cycle

number of finished goods SKUs to grow over time, with generally adverse results. One company I worked with had items in their portfolio that had not sold a single unit for over three years. Another company rented an entire warehouse to store items that should have been considered very slow moving or obsolete. The owner of the company was sure they could be sold at some point, even though no effort was being made to do so. He would not consider labeling them as obsolete, so I created a new category of inventory—glacially slow moving.

Besides managing the product portfolio, ramp-up/ramp-down is essential for managing inventory levels, improving profit, and freeing up cash. Both sides of the product life cycle curve need to be managed closely to make new product introduction more effective and to eliminate unnecessary inventory during the back half of the cycle.

It is also necessary to manage suppliers closely during both ramp-up and ramp-down. Many companies certify suppliers at current production levels without regard to product ramps and new product development. Boeing ran into unprecedented ramp-up of production on its new 737 Max aircraft.[1] Their ramp was very steep and the supplier of the part in question couldn't keep up. That was a perfect example of not managing a supplier well and not including them in the planning processes. This is the essence of Benjamin Franklin's proverb "For want of a nail the shoe was lost."

---

[1] Ostrower (2015).

Inviting Suppliers to the Design Party

Engineering should play a key role in communicating with supplier partners. One technique I've used very effectively is the Supplier Day. This is an event where the top supplier partners (usually 25 or so for small- and mid-market companies) are called in annually for a day of presentations, communication, and relationship development. One of the items on the agenda should be a presentation by design engineering about the products reaching a stage of development where suppliers will be involved in the last steps of design and product roll-out. Not only does this provide important information to the suppliers, but it also gets them excited for the opportunities that lie ahead. It provides a forum for the engineers to develop relationships with the supplier partners and gives suppliers an opportunity to collaborate with other suppliers related to supply chain and new product opportunities.

ACS conducted just such an event for their top 25 suppliers. The unexpected benefit was the opportunity for suppliers to work together to better serve the company. By having sales, engineering, and even accounting present their plans and seek supplier input, the company developed stronger partnerships internally and externally.

Suppliers can also bring key information to the engineering design process if they are included early in the design phase. Keep in mind that suppliers should have very strong knowledge of manufacturing processes, materials, raw materials availability, and other key elements of product and process design. If their technical capabilities are strong, their ability to contribute effectively to product design should also be strong. They might be able to suggest alternative materials that could perform better or reduce costs or both. They are also very familiar with their own production processes and can contribute to design adjustments that will make it easier, faster, or cheaper for them to produce the parts.

Many companies won't include key suppliers because they want to reserve the right to put the parts out for bid to help reduce costs. The problem with that is twofold:

1. Key suppliers for the parts should already be identified, so a general request for proposals (RFP) approach would not be appropriate.

2. The ability to develop relationship costing, which can save from 10 percent to 20 percent or more, would not be possible.

As described in prior chapters, the number of suppliers should be as small as possible, with any given part coming only from one, but with backup to reduce risk. Engineers should work with purchasing and manufacturing engineers to help develop outside suppliers' capabilities to better serve the company.

In one case, by showing the suppliers part drawings early on, they could see which tolerances were key to the design and which could be opened up to let them produce the part more easily. Often, tolerances are called out in general and applied to all dimensions, when, in fact, only some of the dimensions may be critical to the design. By having the suppliers in the room during early design reviews, the changes can be easily made before it's too late.

Another benefit of getting suppliers involved early is that they can begin to design their own internal processes to help get parts into their production cycle quicker. Speed and lead times can be vital to reducing costs and improving delivery, which are two of the primary measures of supplier performance. Helping them be successful is all in the spirit of partnership.

Reference

Ostrower, J. 2015. "Boeing Scrambles to Key Key Part." *Wall Street Journal,* August 21, p. B1.

CHAPTER 8

Your Salespeople Can Be the Best Partners

Operations and sales are in a unique position in the company because sales is the first point of contact with the customer and operations is often the last. Both groups' objectives include customer satisfaction and maximum revenue for the company. The common focus is obvious, but in many companies, the stress between the two groups can be overwhelming. Defining success together and doing everything possible to help the other be successful can dramatically improve revenue and competitive advantage. As VP, Operations, my philosophy with the sales team was that if you sell it, we'll ship it, on time, with excellent quality, at the lowest possible cost. We worked to achieve "perfect orders": right quantity, right time, and right quality, which gave us a highly competitive advantage in the marketplace.

Sales and Operations Planning

The purpose of sales and operations planning (S&OP) is to synchronize sales, operations, supply chain, and capacity management to provide the best possible service and products to the customer, when needed, at the lowest possible cost. While this book is not intended to be a deep dive into S&OP, the process is a great example of how partnerships internally (between sales and operations) and even externally (with customers) can dramatically improve overall performance.

The process spans the entire organization from top management down to the day-to-day activities of sales coordinators and operations schedulers and planners to help assure that customer needs are met. Open communication and trust are at the core of successful S&OP, just like any other successful partnership.

Demand management	Supply chain management
Product management	Inventory management

Figure 8.1 Sales and operations planning building blocks

The building blocks of partnership-based S&OP are demand management, supply chain management, product management, and inventory management (Figure 8.1).

Many companies rely solely on sales forecasting as the cornerstone of S&OP, which causes frustration if the sales department either doesn't provide forecasts or the forecasts are highly inaccurate, which is inevitable because "accurate forecasting" is an oxymoron. Achieving even 80 percent accuracy is quite an accomplishment. While trying to make forecasts as accurate as possible certainly helps, operations should try to become as agile as possible to respond to inevitable shifts in the marketplace.

Many world-class companies use demand planning to help overcome inaccurate forecasts. For instance, Toyota allocates products to their dealers to smooth product flow, which is essential in the Toyota Production System. Proctor and Gamble receive real-time product movement data from Wal-Mart to help them achieve just-in-time product deliveries. Wal-Mart developed radio frequency identification (RFID) to help cut the time from customer purchase to delivery to improve inventory management.

Supply chain management is also an important element of successful S&OP. Knowing your supplier lead times and continuously trying to shorten them can dramatically improve the ability to respond to orders and changes in expected demand, while keeping inventory at a reasonable level. One company I know had materials lead times from suppliers in Asia of four to six months, but their sales forecasts only went out three months, making it very difficult to plan materials flow to fill orders. They had previously focused on maximizing supplier plant efficiencies to cut costs, but that caused missed orders and excess inventory. By bringing supply lead times in line with their three-month sales-planning horizon, the company improved customer service, reduced inventory, and actually improved the cost models with their suppliers. That is a win for everyone, and the result of partnership thinking.

The third building block is product management. Often, new product introduction is not well integrated into S&OP, yet new products can have a direct impact on the flow of goods available for sale. At the same time, keeping older products in the portfolio past their useful life not only increases slow-moving and obsolete inventory, but it also unnecessarily consumes the planners' time in making sure that the products really aren't needed.

The process that I call ramp-up/ramp-down should be part of any S&OP process. Product managers need to plan the anticipated demand, at least in the short term, for new products. Without accurate forecasts, product managers are forced to rely on product history for planning, and new products obviously don't have history. Normally, anticipated demand is part of the product plan, and many companies have key performance measures that track actual to plan and time to first profit for new products. Unfortunately, the rigorous review of old products is often neglected—it's just not as exciting as working with new products. Both ramp-up and ramp-down management are vital to effective S&OP.

The fourth building block for S&OP is inventory management. Knowing what you have and where it is seems pretty obvious, but you would be surprised how many companies don't really know because their inventory is not accurate, or their sales processes drive activity from the wrong distribution center (DC).

I had one client that developed a different product cost depending on which DC the product was shipped from. There was an internal process that suggested which DC should supply the order based on which market was being served, and the planners made sure that there was product on hand in accordance with those sales processes. The problem was that it didn't take long for the customers to figure out that they could buy the same product at a lower price from a different DC. When they insisted on shipment from the lower-cost DC, it threw off the whole planning process. I never cease to be amazed how many buyers are not responsible for logistics costs, so they buy products in a way that reduces product cost while ignoring the principles of total cost of ownership, which includes logistics costs.

One of the key metrics in inventory management is the cost of holding inventory. This cost is comprised of

- Cost of capital
- Cost of facilities and warehousing
- Handling costs
- Racking and other storage equipment
- Obsolescence
- Inventory adjustments
- Insurance
- Taxes

Taking all of these costs into account helps illustrate how expensive having too much inventory is and helps the purchasing team decide whether buying in high volume to get discounts actually saves money in the long run. Over many years of calculating this for both manufacturing and distribution companies, I have found the average cost of holding inventory to be 2 percent to 3 percent per month, which adds up to a whopping 24 percent to 36 percent per year. So, if a buyer was getting a 5 percent discount for buying six months' worth of inventory, they will lose at least 7 percent and possibly as much as 13 percent on the deal.

Data analytics can provide extremely useful information to help understand and stabilize demand. In distribution environments, the turn and earn report can help manage the product portfolio and inventory levels. This report shows the following by part number for the prior 12 months rolling as appropriate:

- Total revenue
- Units sold
- Cost per part

- Total cost
- Margin per part
- Total units currently in inventory
- Total value in inventory at cost
- Inventory turns (inventory divided by total cost)
- Date last sold/used

This report can reveal which parts make or lose money and which ones are cash drains in inventory. Many executives are surprised by how many parts have low or no margin and high inventory.

Communication Makes the Difference

Strong communication between sales and operations is the foundation of S&OP. In addition, many companies include the executive team to help ensure that the company's key strategies and initiatives are supported by the S&OP process. Unfortunately, many companies rely on a weekly or monthly meeting with attendees from all levels in the organization. This meeting often resorts to approval of purchase orders to suppliers, hoping that the materials purchased will be on time while controlling the impact on cash and inventory. Discussion rarely includes more strategic issues like the impact and timing of new product releases, architectural issues such as improving the distribution network design to better serve customers, changes to the supply chain plan in terms of number and location of key suppliers, impacts of major marketing initiatives, financial performance, and so on.

I often recommend a three-tiered structure of meetings (Figure 8.2) in order to focus on issues appropriate to the attendees' level in the organization.

All three levels represent teams, not committees. The members have shared objectives that benefit all members of the team. On committees, each member has his or her own independent agenda, which leads to power plays in an effort to attain one's personal goals at the expense of the group.

At the top level is the executive S&OP team, which includes executives involved in the company's market strategy and those who deal

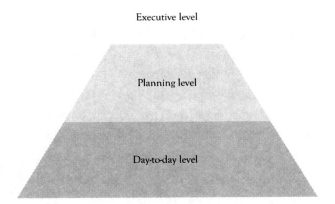

Figure 8.2 Sales and operations planning meeting structure

with cash flow and asset management specifically related to inventory. This usually means the CEO-, CFO-, and the VP-level (or higher) heads of sales, operations, and new product development. This team meets monthly and the agenda includes

- Status of revenue and cash flow for the company as it relates to S&OP
- Status of new product development, new product performance, and new product plans
- Strategic issues related to the supply chain such as whether to regionalize to shorten lead times
- Changes to the distribution network
- Market shifts, both expected and unexpected
- Major customer issues
- Allocation of resources

Key managers may attend this meeting to obtain information and to provide information for decision making, but this meeting doesn't focus on them.

The next level is the planning-level S&OP meeting, which is where the actual S&OP takes place. The attendees are the key managers from sales, operations, accounting/finance, product development, supply chain/purchasing, and quality. The meeting occurs weekly, and key agenda items include

- How to address issues developed in the executive S&OP meeting
- Detailed materials flow issues such as stock status, supply chain interruptions, materials allocation issues and needs, and materials expediting
- Demand management and sales forecasts, including significant changes
- Sales issues such as product promotions, customer problems, demand shifts, and market changes
- Logistics issues such as weather interruptions, dock strikes, other delays, flow issues, and changes in costs/tariff structures
- Any other issues that would impact the timely delivery of product to the customer or the plans used by the supply chain to manage flow

A representative from the executive level should attend to serve as the interface, as needed.

The third level is the day-to-day or ground-level S&OP team. This level includes the key planners from sales and supply chain, usually two people, who meet every day to share any late breaking news of importance. Often, these meetings are the classic "hallway" meetings: informal, typically at someone's desk or in a small conference room. These opportunities to share are what keep the train on the tracks and moving forward as fast as possible. The key here is to support the golden rule of business, "Let there be no surprises." Information sharing on a daily basis allows issues to be identified and often rectified before the next planning-level meeting takes place. Caution should be taken to ensure that the teams don't become completely reactionary and that issues are dealt with within the overall S&OP plan.

Keeping Sales in the Critical Path

Operations has a responsibility to keep sales in the critical path, essentially saying that if sales can sell it, operations can ship it. Keeping the promises that the sales team makes to the customer requires a great deal of agility and flexibility in operations. In the spirit of partnership, sales should only make promises that operations can keep. By managing demand, developing and frequently communicating plans, and working to understand customer needs, operations can become a strategic weapon for the company. Supra's VP, Operations, often visited customers to find out how product packaging impacted usability and quality upon receipt. Often, just showing up had a positive impact on the customer's impression of the company.

One place where sales can help operations provide better service at lower costs is by reducing interruptions caused by order changes. In the world of Lean, there are seven wastes defined by the Toyota Production System: overproduction, waiting, transportation, processing, inventory, motion, and defects. Some people talk about an eighth waste, either the waste of unused knowledge or the waste of unnecessary complexity. However, as I work with manufacturers, distributors, and even in office environments, I see an even greater waste: interruptions.

How often have you seen the boss come into an office and tell someone to drop everything and work on something "more important"? Have you seen salespeople stop production of one order in favor of another, supposedly more important, order? These situations can cause many of the standard seven wastes. For example, interrupted orders get set aside, causing a buildup of work in process, increased inventory, inefficient use of space, and sometimes defects. How about answering phone calls, e-mail, or spending time on social media? Studies show that when a person's thought process is interrupted, it takes up to 20 minutes to become productive again. There is even a term for this, context switching, coined by computer designers to indicate the process of saving and restoring data in an operating system. Designers try to minimize context switches because of how time-consuming they are.

So, if an interruption is a waste, how do you respond to opportunities as they come up? I propose that you always be ready for them, that is, be agile. Be so good at process and productivity improvement that you can respond to almost any request in a very short time and thereby be attentive to the customer's needs. Companies commonly focus on one or two of the process improvement tools in Lean, Six Sigma, Theory of Constraints, and other methods. One company I recently toured focused almost exclusively on setup time reduction. As I walked around, I noticed a shortage of floor space and lots of unused junk scattered throughout the facility. It was so bad they couldn't find room to receive product. If you want to become agile, you can't focus on one or two of the tools, you must do them all.

While there may be instances where the customer needs a response immediately, in most cases, if they can be next in line, that is sufficient, especially if the line is short. Three things will help you keep the line short. First, make sure everything you are doing is important. Activities should be planned, focused, and timely. Planned means that they are scheduled and meet a preset objective. Focused means well-designed activities, usually done subject to standard work or other process discipline. Timely suggests that the step is relatively short and is done just before it is needed.

Second, abide by process discipline. Good process discipline occurs when people follow the rules and avoid tasks that are not compliant with prescribed process or instructions. Standard work is one approach that can help in this regard. Good process discipline helps you "do it right the first time," which is basic to high quality.

Third, think speed. Speed comes from small batch sizes or even flow, which are both vital for just-in-time operations. There is an entire process emerging called Quick Response Manufacturing (QRM), which focuses on cycle time reduction. In many businesses, speed is the key to operations improvement. Eliminating the speed bumps that slow down process cycle time in manufacturing, distribution, and even service operations can greatly enhance operations excellence and customer service.

Reducing interruptions will significantly boost productivity, customer service, and profitability. Eliminate this waste in all aspects of your operations and you will be pleasantly surprised at the improvements. When sales and operations work together to increase agility, operations will help keep sales in the critical path and provide for the level of revenue both teams aspire to.

Communication and trust create the strong foundation for partnerships needed to provide extraordinary customer service. The business impact of strong partnerships between sales and operations include:

- A more strategic view of supply chain management with a focus on the customer
- Reduced order lead times and improved customer service
- Reduced financial impact of slow and obsolete inventory
- Improved cash flow
- Support of company growth and new product initiatives
- Better synchronization of interdepartmental planning processes
- Less stress and conflict between sales and operations

One of the ways to increase communications is to understand why things don't get done. The answer is usually one or more of the following: too many priorities, lack of accountability, and lack of follow-up.

Through strong S&OP, the priority target can be moved effectively when everyone affected picks up their side and moves it together. It's vital to limit the number of priorities to a few; it is much better to move a few things forward a mile than a thousand things forward an inch. The executive S&OP team should set those priorities and the lower teams should focus on execution. People need to know which projects are priorities and why. Once priorities are set, if a new one emerges, an old one should be put on hold, which one of my clients refers to as "putting it in the parking lot." As projects are completed, items from the parking lot can be added to the working list, which solves one of the biggest fears, which is forgetting about the issue.

Another key element is to establish accountability and to follow up. Follow-up often is completely overlooked. In World War II, General Patton once said that many of his officers' biggest failing was that they did not follow up on their orders. If you assign priorities but fail to follow up, people will soon figure out that you aren't really serious and the work won't get done. Holding people accountable and following up ensures that the work gets done, which leads to an agile organization with sales in the critical path.

CHAPTER 9

Employee Partnerships for Increased Profits

An essential partnership for any company is that between the company and its employees. Companies are looking to develop productive, high-quality, loyal employees, and employees want an enjoyable place to work with the opportunity to grow, be challenged, and make more money. Both the company and its employees want to be respected and to benefit from their collective success.

Unfortunately, many companies focus almost exclusively on making the quarterly numbers and cut head count, benefits, and other employee-related expenses, and then wonder why morale is low. The old saying "The beatings will continue until morale improves" is all too true in some companies. I remember seeing on TV that a company executive announced to his employees that the plant was moving to Mexico and they were all going to lose their jobs and then asked them to join him in celebrating the company's success in its new endeavors. What kind of partnership is that?

Many companies seek compliance rather than commitment. Recently I was talking to a VP, Operations, about his role in the organization and how to improve the company's operations. He told me his role was to develop policies and procedures and monitor them for compliance. If compliance wasn't forthcoming, he took action to change behavior, usually through training or discipline.

Can you imagine how excited his people must be about change, how engaged they are in process improvements? They are probably walking on eggshells every moment of the day. While rules should be followed—and there are some instances where compliance is critical, such as dangerous work environments or extremely precise processes—most companies that have a high-compliance culture find that people won't take chances and are afraid to make mistakes. They don't look for opportunities for improvement or cost reduction through problem solving or "do easy" approaches because they're afraid of the discipline that might follow if they stray from established norms.

It's much better to have a workforce committed to everyday improvements, to processes, to their own jobs, and to the business as a whole. Commitment to personal and organizational success creates an environment of excitement, success, and fun. A culture of commitment creates an empowered workforce that will work toward excellence in performance and customer service.

How to Get Employees to Care

For employees to be fully engaged and in partnership with management and others in the company, trust and relationship need to be strong. In many cases, lack of trust can lead to high turnover rates and unionization. On the other hand, strong trust and relationship can yield improved productivity and quality, a strong continuous improvement environment, great customer service, and a team-oriented culture.

It is up to management to set the stage for employee partnerships. The first step for getting employees to care is for you to care about them. Many people have asked me how we started the World Class transformation at Supra Products. To their great surprise, I tell them we painted the lunchroom. I am sure they were expecting me to say something like we conducted training, or we did 5S (a Lean workplace organization technique), or we did a pilot project, or something like that, but instead I had the lunchroom painted and we brought in a new refrigerator and microwave ovens.

When I first came to the company, the lunchroom was dark, dingy, and run-down. The refrigerators were dirty and several of the microwaves did not work. That certainly didn't support the idea that management cared. The lunchroom makeover garnered an interesting reaction from the employees—sort of a "this is different" reaction. I had their attention.

Then I started what I called "a break with Rick." For the afternoon break, I had my secretary randomly select five people from production and the warehouse to take their 15-minute break with me in my office. I brought in frozen yogurt and cookies and we sat around my table and talked. I asked them about themselves and told them about me. Then I asked what things were bugging them and what got in the way of them doing their work. The first group was very guarded, but as word got out that the meetings were fun, the yogurt and cookies were good, and I was very approachable, people started clamoring to take part. The feedback I got was invaluable, and the trust and relationship we established set a solid foundation for the changes ahead.

Then we started the Friday potlucks, when everyone was invited to bring in his or her favorite dish for lunch. We extended it from 30 minutes to one hour and everyone ate together. Eventually, we had to break it in two to accommodate our growth. The food was terrific, several people asked me to taste their contributions, and I soon found bags of cookies, tamales, pot stickers, and other delights on my desk. The team culture we wanted to form was firmly established and the sense of cooperation and trust was strong. Then we started training, doing pilot projects, and initial Lean activities.

The last keystone in the foundation was to foster open communication about the company's financial performance. We were privately held, so the practice for over 30 years had been to keep financial results secret. Interestingly, there was a profit-sharing plan, but there were rarely profits to share and it became a joke: Sales are up, profits are down, sorry, no profit share this quarter. Not only was it not an incentive, but it eroded the employees' trust in management.

As part of our transformation, we did two things: We shared more information with employees, and we taught them how to use it. We knew that most employees could not read a financial statement, so we reduced it to a few key points, which we presented monthly. The first time, we used Monopoly money and gave them an example of how it worked in the categories of revenue, cost of goods sold (materials and labor), overheads (rent, management, building, etc.), and profit. We started with $100 of revenue and ended up with a few dollars of profit. Then we talked about how we could increase profit and what specifically they could do to help.

We improved benefits and pay scales so that they would reap some reward on their efforts. In particular, we started a 401K with high match since management believed that social security alone would not be sufficient for anyone's retirement, and we suspected that most employees were living paycheck to paycheck and weren't saving for retirement. We held investing classes to explain the difference between stocks, bonds, and mutual funds and explained how, with the match, they could make a lot more money without greatly impacting their take-home pay. The 401K had a high participation rate, which kept our plan from being top-heavy, since most of our managers contributed regularly.

By focusing on things that made a real difference to our employees and by helping them develop a sense of trust and relationship with management, we enlisted their wholehearted support for the changes we needed to make to strengthen the company's performance. The improvement was astounding. We grew from $13 million to over $55 million in about five years and went from breakeven (or worse) to over 20 percent profits, while providing our managers and employees with a fun place to work, good pay and benefits, and a sense of satisfaction in their jobs that was unmatched in the community.

Empowered Teams Still Need Direction

One of the legs of the three-legged stool of World Class Manufacturing was "Total Employee Empowerment." The concept of the empowered team has been around since the mid-1980s when the Toyota Production System was experiencing a resurgence in U.S. companies. Teams are an important part of continuous improvement. There are five things you can do to strengthen the teams at your company:[1]

1. Hire for intrinsic traits
2. Provide clear objectives
3. Pay well
4. Give autonomy
5. Focus on progress and improvement

One company I worked with didn't treat their employees as teams or internal partners. The company owners did all of the reviews and determined any raises. They sought only very cursory input from managers

---

[1] Wellins, Byham, and Wilson (1991).

who had little or no role in the process. Some managers didn't even know what their employees were paid. The resulting system provided no incentive and was perceived as very unfair. The employees did not know what to do to earn more and get better reviews. Morale was low and output did not meet the company's needs.

Empowered teams are self-directed in the work they do on a day-to-day basis. They are empowered to make decisions about what and how to do their work. They solve problems, adjust schedules, make output-related decisions, and share some leadership responsibilities. Sometimes, they are even empowered to request (and fire, when necessary) temporary workers, as needed, to improve team performance.

The team leader is the key position on the team. In some companies, this position is rotated among the team members, while in other companies, the team leader is a position achieved through performance and promotion. It is a working leadership position and is not the same as that of a foreman or supervisor. The team leader's role is to drive problem solving within the team.

If you have empowered teams, do you still need managers? Of course. Managers set the vision that the team works to achieve; they provide resources and help develop team leaders; they also set the overall goals and priorities for the teams; and they help resolve conflict between teams. The keywords for managers include support, advice, resolution, goal setting, and development.

One day, when I was VP, Operations, I overheard some strong words out on the shop floor between a production manager and several members of a work cell team. I decided to go and listen in. What I heard was "We are empowered and don't need to listen to you!" Wrong. The issue was one of priorities across customer orders. I stepped in to re-explain the roles of the team and the manager. I made sure the team remained empowered in the areas for which they were responsible and that the manager was empowered in her areas. Once this was cleared up, the issue was resolved and everyone went back to work with a new understanding of how teams worked in our company and how managers set agendas and supported their teams. These sorts of clarifications are continuous in partnerships between managers and teams and build an even stronger culture for the organization.

One of the management's duties is to establish the vision and objectives for the teams. The vision tells them where they are going (the future state) and, most importantly, why. Understanding why you're doing things contextualizes the customer's needs as well as the performance of the company, the team, and the individual. Even in the most difficult circumstances, such as a contentious union environment, understanding why management wants something goes a long way toward developing trust between the partners in the process.

Clarifying Expectations

There are four ways to build trust between the company and employees:

1. Strong leadership
2. Shared vision
3. Culture of openness and collaboration
4. Accountability

Trust is a keystone of partnerships, and without it, performance will always fall short of its potential. Lack of trust indicates that not everyone is working toward the same vision and objectives. Many companies think they have teams, but what they really have are committees; teams have common objectives and a shared vision, while committees have individual objectives that are not in alignment.

In my consulting work, I often interview managers and employees at all levels of the organization. One of my favorite questions is, "At the end of the day, how do you know you did a great job?" The person often looks into space and says something like "I don't know" or "I didn't get into trouble." That is very illuminating but certainly not what I was hoping for. I want to hear, "I helped a customer," "I helped solve a problem," or "I helped a teammate" or something that helps the company meet its objectives.

The key here is that the employees need to know what the objectives are. Any strategy or change initiative starts with a clear vision, which management conveys to the employees. Like light passing through a prism, there is the possibility of refraction at the management level (Figure 9.1), and it is incumbent upon managers to avoid this.

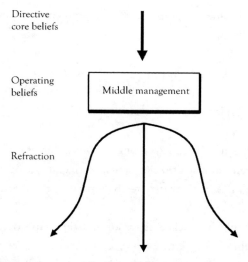

Directive core beliefs

Operating beliefs

Middle management

Refraction

Figure 9.1 Management must convey the vision to employees and avoid refraction

Source: Alan Weiss, Summit Consulting, used with permission.

The vision that management develops should set a clear objective or "future state," as Lean enthusiasts call it, that helps employees know not only where they are going but also why. Employees want to know the why so they can see how it relates to them. Often, the vision goes to middle managers who are busy doing their jobs and they fail to convey the objectives to their employees. When employees know where they are going and why, management's expectations make sense.

Using key performance measures is an effective way to clarify expectations. The measures you use will be directly tied to your organization's long- and mid-term goals. At Supra, we had several measures that never changed:

- Shipped on time (percentage)
- Labor as a percent of sales
- Materials as a percent of sales
- Scrap
- Units shipped by day/week
- Overtime

We tracked some things only until the problem went away:

- Errors
- Quality—first pass yield
- Safety
- Special project-related measures

Many companies track safety, but we found that as our program took hold, there were no lost time accidents, so tracking it became pointless. We did maintain an active safety team, and safety remained important to the organization.

Results should be tracked as trends and the graph trend line should go up when things are getting better and down if they're getting worse. Sometimes we need to change the math so that the lines behave properly. For instance, for materials as a percent of sales to go up, you need to calculate a materials margin. Figure 9.2 is a sample graph.

In this case, the trend is going down, which is not good.

It's also important to display these graphs where everyone can see them. A perfect place is on a wall between the workplace and the lunchroom where everyone walks by every day. Another good place is where the teams have their five-minute stand-ups every day.

At Supra, I made it a point to stop and look at the charts every day. I made sure that people saw me do it, and occasionally, I would ask people to explain to me what was going on with the numbers, which helped them to understand that the numbers are important and that they had better

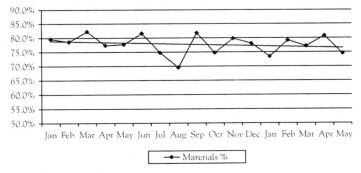

Figure 9.2 Materials margin % of gross sales

understand them. I also had managers discuss the numbers frequently during team meetings.

I also had regular all-hands meetings to express what was going on and to answer any questions. Not only did that reinforce trust, but it also nipped many rumors in the bud.

Can Everyone Win?

The good thing about partnerships is that they are true win/win relationships. For employees, partnerships offer the opportunity for them to

1. Enjoy their work and have fun
2. Understand clearly what is expected
3. Be fairly compensated for their work
4. Be empowered to improve their performance
5. Understand their personal contribution to the team and the company's success

For the company, partnerships with the employees provide

1. A strong workforce
2. High employee loyalty and low turnover
3. Reduced costs of turnover and retraining
4. Highly productive, innovative teams with low costs as a percent of sales
5. Improved profit and growth
6. Reduced failure work and the costs associated with it

This win/win also applies to temporary employees. Everything we have talked about works with a workforce that is supplemented by temporary workers as well. Supra and many other companies have workforces made up of significant numbers of temps, up to 35 percent of the total workforce. Some companies treat the temps as outsiders, which makes it difficult to have a homogeneous workforce. When temps are included in all of the events and team meetings, they become part of the team and will be highly productive, produce high-quality product, and develop a loyalty that can be surprising. When we had to release temps during slower periods at Supra, many of them told their agency not to place them anywhere else so that they'd be available to be recalled.

We also had a unique policy that allowed our team members to fire temps. We were typically very slow to bring temps in and slow to release them because we believed it was fair to the temps and helped cement them as part of our teams. However, if they did not perform, our teams were completely empowered to fire them and request a replacement. Because of this, the teams felt responsible for the temps and tried to help them be successful while also holding them accountable for results.

The amazing part of all of this is that when I came to Supra, there were 61 people on the shop floor. Five years later at over four times the revenue, there were 62 people building essentially the same products. Our labor as a percent of sales (which includes temps and overtime) went from 13 percent to about 3 percent. Our average wage was significantly higher, and our benefits (which were included in our labor cost) were much better. Our labor productivity was greatly improved, which put 10 percent of sales to the bottom line. Talk about win/win!

Building Stairways to Success

Many companies use a pay for skills or job step approach to employee development. Many companies I've been involved with create a range and band approach in which there may be four or five levels of the same job that a person can advance through over the years, which provides a clear path to professional development and higher earnings.

For example, one company had five levels of assembly: Assemblers I through V. The levels were

- Assembler I—on probation (90 to 120 days). Demonstrating the ability to do the basic job and uphold the basic expectations of an employee (arrive on time, cooperate, communicate, work as a team member)
- Assembler II—able to do some of the team's tasks. An active member of the team. Communicates and cooperates in a

positive manner. Builds quality products at a rate that is acceptable to meet the team's needs

- Assembler III—able to do most of the team's tasks and is very proficient in assembling a quality product quickly. Able to oversee temps. Occasionally takes on special assignments and participates actively in improvement projects
- Assembler IV—performs all of the tasks at a high level and can teach others. May act as team leader and supports Assembler Vs in their duties. Measures and tracks key indicators
- Assembler V—supervisor. Conducts performance reviews, schedules work, sets daily expectations, reports to the production manager, and leads improvement activities

In these systems, workers do not have to progress through the levels unless they want to. Pay is capped at the highest level for the band. Even though there is some overlap in the bands for compensation, eventually workers will "cap out" if they do not progress in their skills and value for the company. On the other hand (remember the partnership?) there is no need for a position to be "open" for a person to promote up to a IV. If you were lucky enough to have all IVs, you would be extremely productive and probably have a lower head count over time. It would be an all-star team. I've often wondered why companies cap the number of people in a band, when it can be structured to be positive for both the employee and the company.

This can apply to production, warehouse, engineers, buyers, customer service representatives, accountants, and more. I've seen welders, painters, software developers, and many others in a system like this, with dramatic results for the company and the employees. Isn't that the essence of a partnership with employees?

Reference

Wellins, R., W. Byham, and J. Wilson. 1991. *Empowered Teams.* San Francisco: Jossey-Bass.

CHAPTER 10

Implementing Partnerships

Planning for Partnerships

For partnerships to be successful, they must be part of the company's culture and way of doing business, not just a tool for interfacing with suppliers. Partnership is an attitude that begins at the executive level and permeates the entire organization. It is looking out for the other side's best interests while achieving breakthrough results for yourself. It changes the way an organization thinks and behaves, especially in times of difficulty.

Successful partnerships require a strategy, which must itself be tied to the business strategy. Here are a few questions to ask as you create your partnership strategy:

- What innovations will we need over the next several years to be successful?
- What resources will those innovations require, and do we have those resources now?
- What technical capabilities will we need to obtain or develop?
- How much faster do our processes need to be?
- Which of the needed resources will we develop in-house, and which should we partner to obtain?

Partnership strategy is a pull/push approach like a freight train with locomotives in both the front and back; the front engines pull the train, while the back engines, carefully synchronized with the front, push the train. Using both sets of engines reduces stress on the couplings between cars, reduces friction between the wheels and the track, and uses less energy to move the train. In partnerships, the operations pushes, while the strategy of the business pulls, reducing friction, improving performance, and providing great value to all involved.

Partnership strategy should address the need for speed. In today's business world, speed makes all the difference in competitive situations. Many companies will pay more for products that are delivered faster, and speed is a core competency that partnering can help provide. Much of the philosophy of just-in-time (JIT) is founded on that principle. In the past, JIT was focused on inventory reduction, which would expose the problems and allow for problem solving and continuous improvement.

Asking questions such as "How can we speed things up?" and "What's preventing us from going faster?" can help generate a list of problems that need solving and processes to which you can apply continuous improvement principles. The answers to those questions can also reveal opportunities to work with partners to increase speed.

Once you have your strategy, pick a place to start (e.g., a pilot project) to refine your process and demonstrate success. Rather than selecting the biggest challenge or even the project with the highest return, choose one that is visible and likely to succeed. This project can be internal or external. It is often helpful to prove to outside partners that you have worked on your internal partnerships first to demonstrate your dedication to this effort. They may be more willing to commit when they see you implementing internal partnerships successfully.

Develop an implementation team and create a project vision to share what your objectives are, how you will measure results, and the working environment within which the team will operate. Establish an executive sponsor for the process, usually someone high up who will reinforce the project priorities and resolve resource issues as they come up. Review progress at least every two weeks (the frequency demonstrates that the project is a high priority) and include executives in those reviews. When you can demonstrate success, roll it out more broadly both inside and outside of the organization.

Five Steps to the Altar

There are five steps to getting to the altar for partnerships.

1. Establish a clear vision
2. Identify and prioritize potential partners

3. Develop trust and relationship
4. Develop an agreement
5. Execute the partnership with discipline

The vision provides a clear picture of what you plan to achieve in three to five years. Planning further out than that can be counterproductive because so much can change that the vision becomes unrealistic and people begin to ignore it. Vision accomplishes the following:

- Sets general direction for change
- Provides a means to establish priorities and set goals
- Puts the focus on the big picture: the "why" rather than the "how," which allows for flexibility in the specific approaches used

Using your vision as a yardstick, you can effectively assess a decision, measure an action's relevance and urgency, and apply appropriate resources.

Focus and discipline are required to implement the vision, as well as

1. Clarity of purpose and intended results
2. Metrics for success
3. Accountability to others who frequently review your progress
4. Tools and authority to overcome obstacles
5. Reward, recognition, and commitment

Let your business strategy lead the way as you develop your vision for partnerships. Why are you doing this? If your company is a low-cost producer, your goals for partnerships may be different than if your company focuses on customer service. Understanding who you are as a business will help solidify your vision.

What are the characteristics of a strong vision?

- It provides focus—creating boundaries for change and clarifying what is included and what is not.
- It highlights areas for change—it directs activities toward innovation, cost, quality, attractive workplaces, and more.

- It provides measureable and subjective targets—it can include specific number-based or percentage goals as well as more subjective things such as empowerment and satisfaction.
- It is ambitious—goals should be ambitious yet attainable.
- It should be easily communicated—a strong vision can be explained in just a few minutes.
- It focuses on strengths as opposed to correcting weaknesses.
- It should motivate people—that's what it's all about!

Next, identify and prioritize potential partners. The first place to look is at current partners, especially outside the company, like suppliers and customers. In most cases, current relationships can become partnerships if they are structured properly and the potential partner is willing and has the culture to do so.

An important next step is to distill the candidate pool into a small, core number of candidates. For instance, many of my client companies have a bloated supplier list when we start the supplier partner program, and they often buy the same item from more than five different sources. Not only does this create extra costs in duplicate work, but it often introduces variability in quality. In Chapter 3, we discussed sole sourcing of parts and dual sourcing of technology, but in addition, you should rationalize the supplier base so you have a few, top-performing suppliers as your key partners. Often, 10 or fewer suppliers make up this group and account for 80 percent of your spend. Focus is key here. Spend the majority of your time developing partnerships with the companies that make up 80 percent of your purchasing dollar. Following the Pareto principle (also known as the 80/20 rule) can yield great benefits for your organization and your partners.

Once you have rationalized the potential partners, you can begin improving the relationships. Priorities for improving relationships can be based on a number of factors, such as

- Dollar spend
- Revenue
- Number of units bought/sold
- Relationship to your business strategy
- Contribution to future growth

Focusing on the vital few will help accelerate the partnership. Move a few partnerships forward a mile rather than many forward an inch.

Third, develop trust and relationship through communication, spending time with the partner organization and understanding their goals and objectives. Whether you're partnering with employees, customers, suppliers, or the community, you have to pay your dues by spending time with the potential partner. In Lean lexicon, this is referred to as going to the *Gemba* or point of work to learn about what is going on. You can do the same in partnerships.

As VP, Operations, I learned about our supplier partners by visiting them, touring their facilities, meeting their people, and having casual conversations over meals. The relationships I developed were worth their weight in gold, particularly if there were problems or unexpected opportunities where we needed their cooperation.

Develop an agreement that will guide the partnership. For external partnerships, this agreement should be in a legal format, but not the typical lawyer-generated contract. We covered the memo of understanding (MOU) in a previous chapter and there is a sample in the appendix. For internal partnerships, create an agreement that includes objectives and measures so that both partners will know what they are trying to accomplish and how they will know when it has been achieved.

The Project Vision is an excellent internal tool. It contains a paragraph explaining the vision, specific measures to assess progress, and a description of the working environment such as teams, process discipline, and continuous improvement. Reviewing the vision at the beginning of progress review meetings helps keep everyone on the same page.

The last step in making your partnership official is executing with discipline by having clear objectives, measuring results, and holding people accountable. Companies often make rules but fail to speak up when the rules aren't being followed and, even worse, fail to hold the offenders accountable. Accountability, like company culture, starts at the top; management must enforce the rules quickly and fairly at all levels of the organization.

When I was VP, Operations, there was a bright, young buyer in our purchasing department who did well at his job with one giant exception: He was unbelievably disruptive to the team. I got many complaints about him, but because he seemed so good at buying, I let his behavior slip for months. Finally, I couldn't let it go any further. After coordinating with HR, I called him into my office and fired him. It was ugly, which convinced me I had done the right thing, and after he was out of the building, people came into my office to thank me for taking action. I quickly realized I should have disciplined him months earlier. The team's performance improved almost immediately, and the partnerships between teams strengthened beyond my expectations. If I'd taken action earlier, I could have improved performance and probably lessened the ugliness during the termination. I learned a great lesson.

Getting the Executives Involved

As I've mentioned in previous chapters, it is important to get company executives involved in partnerships for several reasons. First and foremost, since partnerships are really a culture issue and culture starts at the top, executives need to set the cultural tone for the company. Second, change management (Figure 10.1) demands executive sponsors to set the vision that will drive partnerships.

Change often doesn't last long. While everyone begins a new initiative with the best intentions, often the pressures of daily demand divert management attention from the task at hand, and the change initiative begins to founder and eventually fails. Getting executives to be involved and support the initiative from the beginning helps avoid these kinds of failures.

	Past	Future
Cause	Corrective	Proactive
Effect	Adaptive	Contingent

Figure 10.1 Change management quadrant

Keeping It Going

One of my early career bosses used to frequently say, "The golden rule of business is let there be no surprises!" To maintain longevity in partnerships, you must measure progress, which boosts accountability and minimizes surprises. For supplier partners, an active feedback program of supplier scorecards helps them know how they are doing and where they can improve. These scorecards should be reviewed frequently with key suppliers so that there are no surprises.

For employees, give feedback frequently; don't wait for the annual review. In many cases, daily feedback is great. I developed a "Five Minute Stand-up" for all of our production teams with this agenda:

1. Is everybody here?
2. How did we do yesterday?
3. What do we need to do today?
4. Are there any issues/problems that will keep us from reaching our goals?

The first step helped reinforce the team concept—it takes everyone's presence and participation to get the job done. Particularly in Lean environments, work is designed around the team unit, or vice versa in some cases. If the process requires five people, it requires five people. If there are only four on a given day, either the team cannot work, the process will be out of balance, or quality will suffer. Management needs to supplement the team with cross-trained workers or temporary workers who have been adequately prepared to serve on the team. The five-minute stand-up uses peer pressure to encourage people to show up on time, since members have an obligation to be there for their team. Peer pressure is unmatched in establishing the discipline of showing up to work on time.

How they did yesterday and what is needed today tells them the score, which, in most cases, is based a level of expected output: units built, orders processed, or customer problems solved. Normally, a monthly plan can be broken down into weekly and daily buckets to make expectations very clear. In some cases, units of output vary; in most cases, the average provides a meaningful metric. Some companies empower teams to decide if they need to work overtime to meet weekly goals, and often they can tell early in the week if overtime will be needed to hit their numbers.

Asking if there are any issues that will prevent the team from reaching its goals allows the team to voice any concerns they may have. At Supra, managers were accountable for getting resources needed to solve the problem and upholding their side of the partnership. If they couldn't solve it, we had a method to take the issue up the chain to get the resources, including taking it to the CEO if necessary.

Partnerships increase competitive advantage for all of the partners. Not only do financial benefits accrue (sometimes to an extraordinary degree), but working relationships improve and the culture and working environment become positive, enjoyable, and rewarding. Internal and external partnerships provide dramatic results and are the foundation for a long, successful marriage. In today's highly competitive global environment, executives are seeking ways to innovate rapidly to stay on top, and partnerships can be a successful tool to help accelerate profit and growth.

Sample Memo of Understanding

This is a memo of understanding (MOU) for Company 1 of Location to purchase Product Name from Company 2 of Location. This MOU is not a purchase order. It defines in general the terms and conditions that apply to purchase orders issued by Company 1 to Company 2 for goods and services and the overall business relationship between the parties. This MOU will begin on Date, Year, and will automatically renew each year thereafter until terminated by mutual agreement of the parties. Terms and conditions of this MOU are given below.

Forecasts and Purchase Orders

A rolling seven-month forecast will be provided to Company 2 by Company 1. In addition, Company 1 will issue firm purchase orders for the first 90 days of its forecasts. Purchase orders for deliveries outside of 30 days may be rescheduled for up to 45 days for a single product's monthly requirement without cost to Company 1. Reschedules greater than 45 days will be negotiated on a case-by-case basis.

Purchase orders may be canceled by Company 1 contingent upon the following:

- Company 1 will be liable for the material and shipping costs for parts purchased by Company 2 to complete Company 1's purchase order requirements. It is understood that some components used in the manufacture of Company 1's products may have a lead time greater than 90 days and therefore would not be covered by Company 1's purchase order. Company 1 will also be liable for these long lead time components to the degree they are purchased to meet Company 1's forecast requirements. Company 2 will make reasonable efforts to minimize the material cost exposure to Company 1 by following reasonable purchasing practices and by using canceled material on other customer programs and/or returning materials for credit.

- Company 1 will be liable for reasonable nonmaterial costs (exclusive of capacity costs) incurred by Company 2 to complete Company 1's purchase order requirements.

Pricing and Terms

Payment terms are 1% 10 days, Net 30. The general conditions and terms found on Company 1 purchase orders and on Company 1 Kanban releases shall apply. However, if conflicts exist between this MOU and Company 1's purchase orders, this MOU will take precedence.

Quality

The expectation is that the products and services Company 1 receives from Company 2 will conform 100 percent to mutually acceptable quality standards. However, Company 1 will evaluate Company 2's quality monthly, based on incoming receipts and line rejects, and Company 2's product quality must be maintained at 98.5 percent or better, or part of all of this MOU may be terminated by Company 1.

Nonconformance

Company 1 will notify Company 2 when nonconforming materials are received, and Company 2 will initiate corrective actions immediately and submit a corrective action to Company 1 purchasing within five days. Company 2 will credit Company 1 for the cost of all nonconforming products, including shipping costs, or replace with acceptable quality product within a reasonable time.

Delivery

The expectation is that deliveries of Company 2's manufactured product to Company 1 will be 100 percent on time. Company 1 will measure and report Company 2's performance in meeting confirmed purchase order delivery schedules. An unreasonable number of late or disruptive deliveries could result in the cancellation of a purchase order or in the termination of this MOU.

Customer Service

Company 1 will measure Company 2's performance in providing good customer service to Company 1. Company 2's customer service should be maintained at a "preferred" rating level as measured by Company 1's "Supplier Monthly Performance Report" or this MOU could be terminated.

Confidentiality

Company 1's "Supplier Confidentiality and Non-Disclosure Agreement" shall apply.

Modifications and Product Changes

Any changes to this MOU must be mutually agreed upon in writing by authorized representatives from Company 1 and Company 2.

Company 1 must submit all product change requests in writing using a "Change Order Notice." Company 2 will then advise any resulting price variances, lead time changes, tooling costs, and so on associated with the change to Company 1 within a reasonable time. If the purchase price of the product changes, the new price will be effective upon the first invoice after the implementation of the change.

If Company 2 recommends a change to the product that results in a purchase price decrease, Company 2 and Company 1 will share the savings and costs to implement equally. Company 2 shall have no obligation or liability for its recommendations.

Company 1 and Company 2 will meet regularly (three to four times per year) to facilitate the business relationship. In addition, both parties will share industry information, manufacturing techniques, trends of relative ideas that could improve the products and services Company 2 provides, and/or the way business is conducted between the companies.

Duly authorized representatives of Company 1 and Company 2 execute this MOU by signing below:

By: _____   By: _____

Name: _____   Name: _____

Title: _____   Title: _____

Date: _____   Date: _____

Index

OTHER TITLES IN OUR SUPPLY AND OPERATIONS MANAGEMENT COLLECTION

Joy M. Field, Boston College, Editor

- *Better Business Decisions Using Cost Modeling, Second Edition* by Victor Sower and Christopher Sower
- *Improving Business Performance with Lean, Second Edition* by James R. Bradley
- *Lean Communication: Applications for Continuous Process Improvement* by Sam Yankelevitch and Claire F. Kuhl
- *Leading and Managing Lean* by Gene Fliedner
- *Mapping Workflows and Managing Knowledge, Volume I: Using Formal and Tacit Knowledge to Improve Organizational Performance* by John L. Kmetz
- *Mapping Workflows and Managing Knowledge, Volume II: Dynamic Modeling of Formal and Tacit Knowledge to Improve Organizational Performance* by John L. Kmetz
- *Managing and Improving Quality: Integrating Quality, Statistical Methods and Process Control* by Amar Sahay
- *An Introduction to Lean Work Design: Fundamentals of Lean Operations, Volume I* by Lawrence D. Fredendall and Matthias Thürer
- *An Introduction to Lean Work Design: Standard Practices and Tools of Lean, Volume II* by Lawrence D. Fredendall and Matthias Thürer
- *Managing Commodity Price Risk: A Supply Chain Perspective, Second Edition* by George A. Zsidisin, Janet L. Hartley, Barbara Gaudenzi, and Lutz Kaufmann

Announcing the Business Expert Press Digital Library

Concise e-books business students need for classroom and research

This book can also be purchased in an e-book collection by your library as

- a one-time purchase,
- that is owned forever,
- allows for simultaneous readers,
- has no restrictions on printing, and
- can be downloaded as PDFs from within the library community.

Our digital library collections are a great solution to beat the rising cost of textbooks. E-books can be loaded into their course management systems or onto students' e-book readers. The **Business Expert Press** digital libraries are very affordable, with no obligation to buy in future years. For more information, please visit **www.businessexpertpress.com/librarians**. To set up a trial in the United States, please email **sales@businessexpertpress.com**.